# THE ART OF
# LIVING WELL

## A BIBLICAL APPROACH FROM PROVERBS

*Kenth Boa*

## KENNETH BOA & GAIL BURNETT

**NAVPRESS**
BRINGING TRUTH TO LIFE
P.O. Box 35001, Colorado Springs, Colorado 80935

# The Art of Living Well

## A Biblical Approach from Proverbs

### Kenneth Boa
### and Gail Burnett

NavPress
Bringing Truth to Life
P.O. Box 35001, Colorado Springs, Colorado 80935

The Navigators is an international Christian organization. Our mission is to reach, disciple, and equip people to know Christ and to make Him known through successive generations. We envision multitudes of diverse people in the United States and every other nation who have a passionate love for Christ, live a lifestyle of sharing Christ's love, and multiply spiritual laborers among those without Christ.

NavPress is the publishing ministry of The Navigators. NavPress publications help believers learn biblical truth and apply what they learn to their lives and ministries. Our mission is to stimulate spiritual formation among our readers.

ISBN 1-57683-122-1

"Bringing It Home" and "Sharing the Journey" were developed by Terri Hibbard, NavPress.

Cover illustration by Ron Thomas / FPG International

Some of the anecdotal illustrations in this book are true to life and are included with the permission of the persons involved. All other illustrations are composites of real situations, and any resemblance to people living or dead is coincidental.

Unless otherwise identified, all Scripture quotations in this publication are taken from the *New American Standard Bible* (NASB) © The Lockman Foundation 1960, 1962, 1963, 1968, 1971, 1972, 1973, 1975, 1977. The other version used is the *HOLY BIBLE: NEW INTERNATIONAL VERSION* ® (NIV®). Copyright © 1973, 1978, 1984 by International Bible Society. Used by permission of Zondervan Publishing House. All rights reserved. In some instances, italics and font formatting have been altered in the Scripture verses.

Printed in the United States of America

1 2 3 4 5 6 7 8 9 10 11 12 13 14 15 / 02 01 00 99

FOR A FREE CATALOG OF
NAVPRESS BOOKS & BIBLE STUDIES,
CALL 1-800-366-7788 (USA)
OR 1-416-499-4615 (CANADA)

# TABLE OF CONTENTS

ACKNOWLEDGMENTS ................................................................... 7

TO THE SPIRITUAL TRAVELER .................................................... 9

AS YOU STUDY ......................................................................... 10

HOW TO USE THIS GUIDEBOOK ................................................. 11

INTRODUCTION—THE ART OF LIVING WELL ............................... 12

INTRODUCTION TO UNIT 1: OVERVIEW OF PROVERBS 1–9 ......... 13

   Day 1: Introducing Proverbs ...................................................... 14
   Day 2: Examining Proverbs 1:7 .................................................. 18
   Day 3: Understanding Divine Wisdom ......................................... 22
   Day 4: Embracing the Word ...................................................... 26
   Day 5: Exhorting "My Son" ....................................................... 30

INTRODUCTION TO UNIT 2: THE CHARACTER OF THE WISE, PART 1   35

   Day 1: The Wise Are Humble .................................................... 36
   Day 2: The Wise Are Righteous ................................................. 40
   Day 3: The Righteous Make an Impact ....................................... 44
   Day 4: The Righteous Are Blessed ............................................. 48
   Day 5: The Wise Are Teachable ................................................ 52

INTRODUCTION TO UNIT 3: THE CHARACTER OF THE WISE, PART 2   57

   Day 1: The Wise Are Faithful ................................................... 58
   Day 2: The Wise Are Self-Controlled ......................................... 62
   Day 3: The Wise Are Peaceable ................................................ 66
   Day 4: The Wise Are Prudent ................................................... 70
   Day 5: The Wise Seek Godly Counselors ..................................... 74

INTRODUCTION TO UNIT 4: COMMUNICATION AND CHARACTER ...... 79

   Day 1: Words of Instruction ..................................................... 80
   Day 2: Words That Destroy ...................................................... 84
   Day 3: Words That Seduce ....................................................... 88
   Day 4: Words That Edify .......................................................... 92
   Day 5: Words Have Limitations ................................................. 96

INTRODUCTION TO UNIT 5: WISDOM AND WEALTH ..................... 101

   Day 1: Attaining Material Wealth .............................................. 102
   Day 2: Wealth Cannot Satisfy .................................................. 106
   Day 3: Wealth Is Fleeting ........................................................ 110
   Day 4: Our Wealth Is Not Ours ................................................ 114
   Day 5: True Riches ................................................................. 118

APPENDIX A—READINGS FROM PROVERBS ............................... 123

APPENDIX B—GOD'S PLAN OF SALVATION ................................. 135

BIBLIOGRAPHY ...................................................................... 139

# ACKNOWLEDGMENTS

Many thanks from Ken to Professor Bruce Waltke, whose teaching provided the original inspiration for many of the concepts presented in this book.

Many thanks from Gail to pastors Cleo Watts, John Wood, and Brad Getz. And many thanks to the New Creations class for working through the pilot studies for us.

# To the Spiritual Traveler

Suppose when you were small, your father had held a book in his hands and said, "When you are old enough, I'm going to give you this book. This is a book about truth, written by the wisest among men. For centuries it has withstood the scrutiny of great scholars, but none has ever proven it wrong. This book holds the secrets to all of life's challenges!

"Now remember, my child, although truth is ancient, it is also timeless. Therefore, these words are just as relevant today as when they were first spoken some three thousand years ago. How eager I am to give this book to you! It will guide you rightly and teach you to be wise. It will touch every facet of your life as it speaks of humility and pride, justice and vengeance, work and laziness, wealth and poverty, friends and neighbors, love and lust, anger and strife, masters and servants—even life and death. Yes, some day, when you are old enough . . ."

You know, I'll bet you couldn't wait to get your hands on that book! How could any child resist such allure? It sounds like a page right out of some mystical fantasy, doesn't it? Yet every description rightly relates to the book of Proverbs. Proverbs is the wisdom of God revealed to us through the prophets and sages (the wise men and women of the Old Testament) and through the life of Christ.

Why, then, do most of us grow up more eager to learn to drive a car than to navigate our lives? Perhaps it's because the value of living our lives by the wisdom of God was not pressed upon us in our youth. But good news—it's not too late! We can begin right now to understand the deep truths of God. Follow God's command from Proverbs 4:5, "Acquire wisdom! Acquire understanding! Do not forget, nor turn away from the words of my mouth."

If you will apply yourself to a disciplined study of the Word of God, you can trust God to reveal Himself and His ways and to give you His eternal perspective so you can see beyond your own limitations. My desire in ministry is to help you learn to observe the events of life and from them gain understanding and discernment. I want to lead you to the Source of truth, so you'll be able to act instead of react and to act *intelligently*—to think things through in relation to God's commands and to His revelation of Himself. Although there is tremendous depth to Proverbs, this Bible study represents only the high points. The goal for this study is to help you commit some of God's truths to memory and to whet your appetite for a life pursuit of wisdom.

—Ken Boa

# As You Study

Spiritual maturity begins with a diligent study of the Word of God. The more you take in and live out, the more you grow in Christlikeness. There's no substitute for spending time in the Word. Time, however, is a diminishing resource in our complex society; and schedules are rarely routine for anyone.

To help address these issues, Dr. Boa and I have developed what we call the GUIDEBOOK series. Guided tours carry people to places of interest, providing information from experts along the way. People take guided tours for a number of reasons. Sometimes they don't know where to go. Sometimes they want more information. Sometimes their time is limited. Sometimes their understanding is limited. In all cases, they need a guidebook.

The GUIDEBOOK series is aptly named. The workbooks are vehicles and we (your tour guides) are longtime Bible teachers and writers. Dr. Boa, in fact, is a theological expert. As we guide you through Proverbs 1–9 we'll be drawing your attention to key verses within the book as well as to other related passages in Scripture. These passages are significant because of their relationship to something of greater importance; namely, God's plan of salvation.

To help you get the most out of your journey, read the suggestions in the adjacent column before you go on. We hope you'll enjoy *The Art of Living Well: A Biblical Approach from Proverbs*. Now, buckle your seat belt. We're ready to go!

—Gail Burnett

## Getting the Most from Your Study

1. **Begin with prayer.** You can gain information on your own, but only God can reveal truth.

2. **Do not read commentaries on Proverbs until you have finished the entire study.** Self-discovery of biblical truth is exciting. It makes the Word of God come alive and also helps you retain what you've learned.

3. **Make sure you understand the structure of this GUIDEBOOK before you begin.** (Explanations are found on the following page.)

4. **Do not skip over directions to read the referenced Scriptures.** The text that follows may not make sense if you have not first read the Scripture passage(s).

5. **Be sure to write your answers to the study questions in the space provided.** Repetition and space for content interaction have been included to help you retain the material. Your answers will be confirmed in subsequent readings. These answers are intended to reinforce what you've already read and written.

6. **Work on this study every day of the week.** Begin the first day of your study week by reading the "unit introduction" page. Work through the Daily Excursions over the next five days, then end your week with review and Scripture memory. You may want to preview "Sharing the Journey" if you are using this study with a group.

7. **Read the articles and suggested Daily Readings in the optional Side Tours, even if you don't have time to do the activities.** The articles and readings are important, and they can be read in a few minutes.

8. **During your day, meditate on what you've learned.** Most Daily Excursions can be completed in less than twenty minutes, but they are "tightly packed." Reflecting on your observations allows biblical truths to expand your understanding and to take shape in your life.

# How to Use This GuideBook

## Instructional Design©

GUIDEBOOKS are self-contained, interactive Bible studies. These studies are primarily inductive; that is, they lead the reader to related Scriptures throughout the Bible so that he or she might experience the joy of self-discovery as revealed by the Master Himself. Therefore, in addition to Scripture references from the key texts, topics are supported by the whole counsel of God. Other outside material and additional Scripture references are included in "For further study."

Each GUIDEBOOK includes five study units divided into five **Daily Excursions**. Most Excursions take about twenty minutes to complete. No additional reference materials are needed. To complete the optional Side Tours, a Bible and a concordance are sometimes needed. Each unit ends with a session plan (Sharing the Journey) for group use in a Bible study, small group, or Sunday school class. (The leader will need to have a flipchart or board and markers or chalk available. All questions and activities should be adapted to best suit the needs of the group members.) While this section is intended for group use, you also can benefit from doing the activities on your own.

## Page Description

GUIDEBOOKS are designed for open, two-page viewing. Each page is divided into two columns, a wide inside column and a narrow outside column, as shown below. Daily Excursions include Bible teaching, related questions, life application (Bringing It Home), and Bible reading. The outside columns contain related Road Map and Side Tour options. At the end of each unit, it is suggested that the reader select one verse from the weekly reading to memorize.

The **Road Map** includes all Bible verses referred to in the Daily Excursions, except for lengthy study texts. (These are provided in appendix A). Scriptures in the Road Map are linked to reference numbers in the Daily Excursions and numbered consecutively throughout the GUIDEBOOK. Unless otherwise noted, all Scripture passages are from the *New American Standard Bible*.

Within quoted Scriptures, **ellipses** (. . .) indicate where portions of text have been omitted (due to space constraints) without compromising the meaning. The verses provided include the essential information for your study; however, you will benefit from reading the full text from your Bible.

The **Side Tours** contain optional reading and Scripture references related to Language & Literature, History & Culture, Bible Study Techniques, Cross References, and Points of Interest (including life illustrations). All Side Tours are referenced in the text and numbered consecutively (preceded by "T") throughout the GUIDEBOOK. For example, the notation [T1] will follow the appropriate text in the Daily Excursion, and this same notation will appear in the adjacent Side Tour column. Because the Scriptures listed in Side Tours are not printed in this GUIDEBOOK, they must be looked up in a Bible.

**Personal Experiences** of the authors are differentiated by their names in parentheses.

---

| ROAD MAP | DAILY EXCURSION |
| --- | --- |

**DAY 1**

**EXAMINING PROVERBS AS LITERATURE**

**"PROVERBS 1**
1 The proverbs [mashal] of Solomon the son of David, king of Israel:
2 To know wisdom and instruction, To discern the sayings of understanding,
3 To receive instruction in wise behavior, Righteousness, justice and equity;

What defines a proverb? The Hebrew word for "proverb" is transliterated[T1] *mashal*, which means "a discourse or a parable." *Mashal* comes from a root word that means "to be similar or parallel; to represent; to be like or be compared to." The book of Proverbs uses comparisons as its primary literary device. A proverb may show how one

---

| DAILY EXCURSION | SIDE TOURS |
| --- | --- |

**BRINGING IT HOME . . .**
1. Look back at your life—as a child, a teen, and a young adult. Also look at your life now. At what point, if any, did you make a choice to reject being naive and foolish and to embrace wisdom? In what ways does that choice still impact your life today?

**HISTORY & CULTURE:**[T3]
AUTHORSHIP—King Solomon, son of David, did not write all of the proverbs, but his work makes up the greater part of the book. Solomon was an observer and a seeker of knowledge. Not only was Solomon's knowledge encyclopedic, his understanding and discernment were such that his

# INTRODUCTION—THE ART OF LIVING WELL

Proverbs deal with the details of living where decisive elements of character are developed and exposed. Proverbs are concise illustrations based on experiences common to humankind. They are easily understood maxims backed up by universal principles with widely ranging applications.

A good definition of a proverb is this: *A simple illustration that exposes a fundamental reality about life.*

The book of Proverbs is a compilation of thought processes and behaviors that distinguish the wise from the foolish. Proverbs offer wise counsel based on the collective experiences of those who have learned a fundamental truth worth passing on to future generations. Living the wisdom of Proverbs is an art—*The Art of Living Well.*

Before we begin this study, there are several things to remember about Proverbs. First, the maxims in Proverbs are universally true and applicable to most cases, but there is room for deviations. Proverbs are not promises of God. Rather they are keenly observed and divinely interpreted patterns of cause and effect in human behavior. Proverbs are totally valid, highly reliable, and typically repeatable. Nevertheless, God is at liberty to intervene and alter those patterns in any way He sees fit; He will do so when our best interest is at stake.

Second, we must carefully read and interpret what these maxims are saying. Some people read what they want Scripture to say and then get angry at God when He doesn't deliver the way they have in mind. If in our own lives we find deviations from principles expressed in Proverbs, we should first go back and read what the verse really says and then examine the truth of how our situation fits that principle. We should go to God for clarity and wisdom, but we must not rail against Him as if He failed to keep a promise.

These two cautions do not lessen the value of Proverbs, nor do they diminish the wisdom of following them. Indeed, Proverbs gives timeless insights; and even today they offer us incredible predictability of outcome. The goal for studying Proverbs is to help us benefit from truths that have stood the test of time by incorporating them into our lives.

## JOB'S DISCOURSE ON WISDOM

But where can wisdom be found? And where is the place of understanding? Man does not know its value, nor is it found in the land of the living. The deep says, "It is not in me"; and the sea says, "It is not with me." Pure gold cannot be given in exchange for it, nor can silver be weighed as its price. It cannot be valued in the gold of Ophir, in precious onyx, or sapphire. Gold or glass cannot equal it. . . . Coral and crystal are not to be mentioned; and the acquisition of wisdom is above that of pearls. . . . Where then does wisdom come from? And where is the place of understanding? Thus it is hidden from the eyes of all living, and concealed from the birds of the sky.

God understands its way; and He knows its place. For He looks to the ends of the earth and sees everything under the heavens. When He imparted weight to the wind, and meted out the waters by measure, when He set a limit for the rain, and a course for the thunderbolt, then He saw it and declared it; He established it and also searched it out.

And to man He said, "Behold, the fear of the Lord, that is wisdom; and to depart from evil is understanding."
(Job 28:12-18,20-21,23-28)

# INTRODUCTION TO UNIT 1
## OVERVIEW OF PROVERBS 1–9

*Destination: To understand the foundational principles given in Proverbs 1–9 and begin apply-ing them to everyday life.*

When I (Gail) was a child, about the worst thing the average teenager did was to cheat on his or her exams. Therefore, from a very early age, my parents grilled me on the evils of cheating until I came to think that people were born with an innate knowledge of that sin. I knew I'd fare far better to flunk the whole year than to ever be caught looking on someone else's paper.

When my children were young, drug use was a serious teen problem and a great concern to parents. Therefore, I began early with "the talks" about the evils of drug use and about its perilous impact on health, happiness, and hopes for the future. By high school, my children were so saturated with home-grown, antidrug campaigns that even friendships with drug users were never a problem (and I thank God for that). But apparently my focus on drugs came at the expense of dealing with other issues; for I learned from both my now-adult children that each had held a very casual attitude about cheating in high school. Both knew cheating was wrong, of course; but since "everyone else did it," each thought the offense to be about equal to chewing gum in class.

I didn't even ask my children if they had ever been guilty of cheating—I was too appalled at their thinking! As I reflected upon all my years of "momisms," however, I couldn't recall one single discussion with them on the importance of not cheating in school. Apparently I presumed (from the strength of my parents' imposed values) that the taboo of cheating was obvious. It wasn't! I learned an important lesson through that experience—*all* values, ethics, and morals must be spoken repeatedly and modeled consistently if our children are to grow in wisdom.

The essence of Proverbs 1–9 is developing a heart for receiving wisdom through the repetition of important teaching in order to develop a heart for wisdom in others. These preparatory chapters of Proverbs are covered in *Pursuing Wisdom,* the first book in this series. *Pursuing Wisdom* focuses on the source of wisdom and on wisdom as it relates to salvation. Because some of the information from Proverbs 1–9 is basic or foundational to understanding the practical and behavioral aspects of the rest of Proverbs, these principles are included in unit 1 of this study. If this is the first GUIDEBOOK you have used, you will find unit 1 to be a fast-paced overview of Proverbs 1–9. While *The Art of Living Well* stands on its own, we recommend that you complete *Pursuing Wisdom* before beginning this study. If you have completed *Pursuing Wisdom*, unit 1 serves as a helpful review.

Living well begins by attaining wisdom. As you start your journey, make a commit-ment to yourself to be diligent and to complete each Daily Excursion as thoroughly as possible. May you heed Solomon's admonition, "The beginning of wisdom is: Acquire wis-dom; and with all your acquiring, get understanding" (Proverbs 4:7). You will be rewarded richly from the truths of God's Word.

# DAY 1

## INTRODUCING PROVERBS

### PROVERBS AS LITERATURE

A proverb is a discourse or a parable that explains primarily by comparing or by contrasting behaviors or characteristics. Proverbs are concise, clear, complete, catchy statements that offer universal truths. They are found in all languages; therefore, they are not unique to the Bible.

### DATE, AUTHOR, RECIPIENTS, AND PURPOSE

The content in the book of Proverbs was written or transcribed between 931 B.C. and 700 B.C. Minor contributors include King Hezekiah, Agur (chapter 30), and King Lemuel (chapter 31).

According to Proverbs 1:1,[1] who is the principal author of Proverbs?

To whom are these words of wisdom addressed, according to verses 4-5?[1]

Solomon's intent was to document words of wisdom so that future generations could more keenly develop their moral awareness, ability to discern, and intellect. His purpose for writing is spelled out in Proverbs 1:2-6.[1] Read these verses and complete in your own words the purpose statements below:

To know

To discern

To receive

To give

To understand

---

**[1]PROVERBS 1**

1 The proverbs of Solomon the son of David, king of Israel:

2 To know wisdom and instruction, to discern the sayings of understanding,

3 To receive instruction in wise behavior, righteousness, justice and equity;

4 To give prudence to the naive, to the youth knowledge and discretion,

5 A wise man will hear and increase in learning, and a man of understanding will acquire wise counsel,

6 To understand a proverb and a figure, the words of the wise and their riddles.

7 The fear of the LORD is the beginning of knowledge; fools despise wisdom and instruction.

The meanings of the preceding five verbs are more passive or bland in the English translations than they actually are in the Hebrew language. The Hebrew understanding of attaining wisdom involved intensive and aggressive engaging of the mind, will, and spirit. Consider these definitions:

"To know" *(yada)* means "to know with certainty."

"To discern/understand" *(bin)* means "to diligently consider and investigate."

"To receive" *(laqach)* means "to seize or capture."

"To give" *(nathan)* means "to commit or assign."

## KEY WORDS AND CONCEPTS

In essence, all of Proverbs is about the value of wisdom and instruction and the consequences of wise and foolish behaviors. Let's look at each of these key words and their transliterations in more detail.[T1]

"Wise" or "wisdom" in the Hebrew language is transliterated *chokmah* (Proverbs 1:2). *Chokmah* carries the idea of gaining skill. In Proverbs, this skill is the art of living a life endowed with the wisdom of God. Wisdom in Proverbs relates to divine truths applied to our daily lives; that is, to the visible outworking of moral acumen, practical righteousness, and integrity.

"Instruction" in Hebrew is transliterated *musar* (1:2), meaning "to discipline, to correct." *Musar* also means "admonishment, correction, reproof, chastisement."

"Fools" or "the foolish" described in the Proverbs come from four different Hebrew words that differentiate among degrees of foolishness:

The "naive" or "simple" are the *pethim*—the aimless, uncommitted, open to suggestion (1:4). *Pethim* comes from the root word *pathath*, meaning "spacious" or "wide open."

The "fools" or "foolish" may be either the *kesilim* who are spiritually dull and insensitive to wisdom (1:22) or the *evilim* who oppose spiritual matters, love folly, and despise wisdom and instruction (1:7).

**STUDY TECHNIQUE:**[T1]
WORD STUDIES—In literature, the original meaning(s) of repeated words or phrases is key to understanding the text. In Bible study, concordances and lexicons are used to look up words in their original language, to determine the meaning within the culture and time period, and to discover root words and etymologies (the origin and evolution of a word, which sheds light on its meaning).

The Hebrew and Aramaic languages of the Old Testament and the Greek language of the New Testament all use a different alphabet. Thus, words listed in concordances and lexicons are *transliterated* into English; that is, they are spelled phonetically using the English alphabet. Key Hebrew words from Proverbs are shown in brackets in the following verses:

1:2-7  To know *[yada]* wisdom *[chokmah]* and instruction *[musar]*, to discern *[bin]* the sayings of understanding, to receive *[laqach]* instruction in wise behavior, righteousness, justice and equity; to give *[nathan]* prudence to the naive *[pethim]*, to the youth knowledge and discretion, a wise man will hear *[shama]* and increase in learning, and a man of understanding will acquire wise counsel, to understand *[bin]* a proverb and a figure, the words of the wise and their riddles. The fear *[yirah]* of the LORD is the beginning *[reshith]* of knowledge *[daath]*; fools *[evilim]* despise wisdom and instruction.

2:6  For the LORD gives wisdom; from His mouth come knowledge and understanding *[tebunah]*.

Concordances are based on particular translations of the Bible. The well-known *Strong's Exhaustive Concordance*, for example, is based on the King James Version. This study uses text from the New American Standard Bible (NASB). A *New American Standard Exhaustive Concordance of the Bible* is published by Holman Bible Publishers. Various concordances and lexicons are also available on computer disk.

²EXODUS 31

1-6 Now the LORD spoke to
Moses, saying, "See, I have
called by name Bezalel. . . . And
I have filled him with the Spirit
of God in wisdom, in understanding, in knowledge, and in
all kinds of craftsmanship, to
make artistic designs for work
in gold, in silver, and in
bronze, and in the cutting of
stones for settings, and in the
carving of wood, that he may
work in all kinds of craftsmanship. . . . and in the hearts of all
who are skillful I have put
skill, that they may make all
that I have commanded you."

³PSALM 78

1-8 Listen, O my people, to
my instruction; incline your
ears to the words of my mouth.
I will . . . utter dark sayings of
old, which we have heard and
known, and our fathers have
told us. We will not conceal
them from their children, but
tell to the generation to come
the praises of the LORD, and His
strength and His wondrous
works that He has done.
For He established a testimony in Jacob, and appointed a
law in Israel, which He commanded our fathers, that they
should teach them to their
children, that the generation to
come might know, even the
children yet to be born, that
they may arise and tell them to
their children, that they should
put their confidence in God, and
not forget the works of God, but
keep His commandments, and
not be like their fathers, a stub-
born and rebellious generation,
a generation that did not prepare
its heart, and whose spirit was
not faithful to God.

The "scoffers" or "scorners" in Proverbs are the *litsim* (1:22). These are cynics full of pride and arrogance. They hold in contempt anyone who has submitted to God's will and rule.

The distinguishing features among the types of fools illustrate the progressive decline of those who resist the call of wisdom. These distinctions will be more meaningful later on in our study.

## THE SOURCE OF WISDOM

Wisdom was a subject of Old Testament writings long before Solomon was born. Wisdom is first mentioned[T2] in Exodus 28 when Moses consecrated the priesthood and supervised the construction of the tabernacle in the wilderness.

Read Exodus 31:1-6,[2] noting the context.[T3] What specific things did Bezalel receive from God?

By what means did Bezalel receive these things?

In all our human effort, we could never attain divine wisdom because such wisdom rests on the work of God's Spirit. At the same time, we have a responsibility to investigate God's Word, seize His revelation, and apply those things we learn to our lives. Like playing an instrument, the skill of wise living (living well) is increased by discipline and diligence. If we would be wise, then we must both rely on God and exert personal effort toward stretching our life skills. We also must be wholly teachable and actively involved in wisdom's pursuit.

In addition to gaining wisdom, we are required to impart wisdom. Read Psalm 78:1-8.[3] Briefly summarize what future generations are to be told.

Which family member is specifically responsible to teach the children about God?

In Israel, priests imparted the Law, prophets communicated divine words and visions, and sages or elders counseled the people and taught schools of wisdom (an institution that has virtually vanished today). The most fundamental resource for passing down wisdom, however, was the family; parents and grandparents imparted wisdom to the children. Scripture, in fact, gives fathers specific responsibility for teaching their children about God. When fathers, and mothers as well, fail to fulfill their role as spiritual teachers, the entire society suffers. As believers we can be spiritual parents to those outside our physical families.

## BRINGING IT HOME . . .

1. Ask God to reveal to you any areas of your life (relational, emotional, physical, mental, spiritual) where you know what is right, but you are not applying wisdom. Record what He shows you.

2. What specific changes in thought, action, or habit do you need to make?

3. Ask God for the strength to make these changes.

## STUDY TECHNIQUE:[T2]
PRINCIPLE OF FIRST MENTION—One way to gain insight on a word's fuller meaning is to look at the context surrounding that word's introduction in Scripture. Wisdom's source and its association with skill are impor-tant components in understanding the Hebrew concept of wisdom as described in Proverbs.

## STUDY TECHNIQUE:[T3]
CONTEXT—Context rules when interpreting meaning. Context in Scripture refers to the bigger picture or vision surrounding a word, verse, chapter, or book of the Bible. The larger context includes things such as the history, culture, time, setting, government, and particular circumstances that influence the author and his writing. The more immediate context includes the verses, subjects, key words, concepts, and doctrinal issues that surround the verses of interest. The full expression of any text can be found *only* within the whole of the idea being presented. This is why context is critical to correct interpretation of Scripture.

## DAILY READING
Read Proverbs 1:8-22. Mark the verse that stands out most to you today.

**[4]PROVERBS 1**

7  The fear of the LORD is the beginning of knowledge; fools despise wisdom and instruction.

**[5]JEREMIAH 8**

9  The wise men are put to shame, they are dismayed and caught; behold, they have rejected the word of the LORD, and what kind of wisdom do they have?

**[6]1 CORINTHIANS 3**

18-21  Let no man deceive himself. If any man among you thinks that he is wise in this age, let him become foolish that he may become wise. For the wisdom of this world is foolishness before God. For it is written, "He is THE ONE WHO CATCHES THE WISE IN THEIR CRAFTINESS"; and again, "THE LORD KNOWS THE REASONINGS of the wise, THAT THEY ARE USE-LESS." So then let no one boast in men.

# DAY 2
## EXAMINING PROVERBS 1:7

Proverbs 1:7[4] is key because it sums up the dominant theme that runs through the entire book of Proverbs. Before we begin, read Proverbs 1:7 and briefly note your initial thoughts on the fear of the Lord or the knowledge of truth.

## CONTRASTING THE WISE AND THE FOOLISH

Proverbs 1:5[1] refers to the "wise" and "understanding." These are people who are rightly related to God; they thoughtfully approach life and seek God for insight on the things they observe. Their pursuit of divine counsel is rewarded with an uncommon sense—a sense that remains wholly dependent upon God for the knowledge of truth. Read Jeremiah 8:9[5] and 1 Corinthians 3:18-21.[6]

Why are the wise men put to shame?

What does God think about the wisdom of the world?

What are some examples of contemporary "wisdom"?

Solomon's writings addressed people with both youthful and innate foolishness (the naive) as well as people who were willfully ignorant of God's ways (the fools and the scoffers).

In what ways are those who are youthful and naive (*pethim*) different from those who scoff (*litsim*) at the things of God? (Refer to pages 15 and 16 if needed.)

Why do you think fools despise wisdom and instruction?

The naive and the scoffers are very different groups. The naive (*pethim*) in Proverbs 1:4[1] are not foolish because they have rejected God but because they have not yet encountered and accepted Him as Lord. The *pethim* portray all of us at some point in our youth. The fools in Proverbs 1:7,[4] however, are the *evilim*. These are men and women who have been exposed to divine instruction, have rejected it, and have therefore suffered the consequences; namely, they've grown *more* foolish. Had they chosen the way of wisdom, however, God would have begun their instruction with a startling revelation of Himself.[T4]

### THE FEAR OF THE LORD

According to Proverbs 1:7[4] what is the starting point for attaining wisdom?

A personal encounter with Almighty God results in a holy fear of the Lord. Fearing the Lord is reverencing God and seeing Him with awe. But fearing God also includes the recognition that God is a God of wrath as well as a God of compassion; He's a God of justice as well as a God of mercy. The Hebrew word for "God fear" is *yirah*. *Yirah* relates to piety, religion, and worship, but it literally means "to be afraid, to revere, to dread, to be terrified." *The fear of the Lord, then, is the heart-stopping realization of God's glory, majesty, and power, and of His right to absolute sovereignty over His creation.*

All who have personally encountered God have fallen on their faces in fear and in wonder that One so mighty would invite them to live in relationship with Him.

What do you think is the difference between knowing about God and fearing God?

---

**HISTORY & CULTURE:[T4]**

ENCOUNTERS WITH GOD—God physically revealed Himself to people in a number of Old Testament encounters—to David, Daniel, Job, Moses, and others. Many of these encounters involved the "Angel of the Lord" who (if He accepted worship) was, in fact, the "preincarnate Christ," that is, God the Son before (pre) He became flesh (incarnate) in the person of Jesus. These appearances are called *theophanies*.

Christ also revealed Himself in His glory to John (Revelation 1:9-18). In each instance, these Bible heroes fell on their faces in fear. If we don't fear the Lord, it means, spiritually, we've never seen His glory.

*For further study:*
Genesis 18
Judges 6 and 13
1 Chronicles 21:16
Daniel 8:1,15-17

[7] **2 TIMOTHY 3**

6-7 For among them are those [false teachers] who enter into households and captivate weak women weighed down with sins, led on by various impulses, always learning and never able to come to the knowledge *[epignosis]* of the truth.

[8] **2 TIMOTHY 2**

24-26 And the Lord's bondservant must not be quarrelsome, but be kind to all, able to teach, patient when wronged, with gentleness correcting those who are in opposition, if perhaps God may grant them repentance leading to the knowledge of the truth, and they may come to their senses and escape from the snare of the devil.

[9] **1 CORINTHIANS 2**

14-16 But a natural man does not accept the things of the Spirit of God; for they are foolishness to him, and he cannot understand them, because they are spiritually appraised . . . For WHO HAS KNOWN THE MIND OF THE LORD, THAT HE SHOULD INSTRUCT HIM? But we have the mind of Christ.

[10] **2 TIMOTHY 3**

15 From childhood you have known the sacred writings [Scriptures] which are able to give you the wisdom that leads to salvation through faith which is in Christ Jesus.

## THE BEGINNING OF KNOWLEDGE

According to Proverbs 1:7, "The fear of the LORD is the *beginning* of knowledge" (emphasis added). The Hebrew word for "beginning" is *reshith*, meaning "topmost, summit, headwaters." The fear of the Lord is not a religious or doctrinal platform upon which we assemble facts about God. The fear of the Lord opens the channel through which divine knowledge flows to us from the very fountainhead of truth.

## THE KNOWLEDGE OF TRUTH

All knowledge is built on information (sensory as well as factual). But even accurate information will not lead to the knowledge of truth unless it is rightly discerned and processed. Read about the students of certain so-called gospel teachers in 2 Timothy 3:6-7.[7]

What were these women always doing?

What always eluded them?

Why? What was their condition?

Sin, false teaching, and impulsiveness detracted the students from discerning truth. In 2 Timothy 3:7[7] the Greek word used for "knowledge" (of truth) is *epignosis*. It means "to know exactly; to recognize and perceive." *Epignosis* has to do with making the right conclusions from the available information to arrive at truth. Likewise, the Hebrew word for "knowledge" in Proverbs 1:7[4] is *daath*, meaning "that which is known; truth." By human reasoning, none of us can tell truth from error. We must evaluate everything we hear and learn, therefore, against the plumb line of God's Word, trusting the Holy Spirit to reveal truth to us. Wisdom is the outworking of *epignosis*. It is the knowledge of truth applied to our lives.

Read Proverbs 1:7[4] again, then read 2 Timothy 2:24-26.[8] What precedes knowledge in these passages?

Proverbs 1:7

2 Timothy 2:24-26

Both the fear of the Lord and repentance must precede the knowledge of truth. Read 1 Corinthians 2:14-16.[9] Why can't natural man accept the things of the Spirit?

What is the source of the wisdom that leads to salvation according to 2 Timothy 3:15?[10]

By the Spirit and God's Word, believers have access to the mind of Christ, which enables them to appraise all things. Those not made new in Christ, on the other hand, can neither understand nor accept the things of God. If in your deepest heart you find the things of God to be foolish, then perhaps you should ask God to reveal the truth about your relationship to Him. Ask God for a deep and abiding revelation of Himself that you might become wise unto salvation and receive the benefits of fearing the Lord.[T5]

## BRINGING IT HOME . . .

1. Our personal response to God and His Word affects every area of our lives. In your heart, what is your view of God? the Scriptures? His people?

2. Listed below are several traits of wise men and women. Check each one that is true of you.
   - ☐ I have a reverence and awe of God.
   - ☐ I know that, apart from faith in Christ, I am unable to understand the mind of God.
   - ☐ I have placed trust in Christ alone for forgiveness and for spending eternity with God.
   - ☐ I view the Bible as God's Word.
   - ☐ I recognize God's right to arrange or rearrange the circumstances of my life for His purposes.

3. Read Proverbs 9:10 from appendix A. If you were not able to check all of the above statements, ask God to search your heart and reveal what is holding you back. Then seek the counsel and prayer of your pastor, small-group leader, or a mature Christian friend.

## CROSS REFERENCES:[T5]
BENEFITS OF FEARING THE LORD—

**Psalms 25:12-14:** Who is the man who fears the LORD? He will instruct him in the way he should choose. His soul will abide in prosperity, and his descendants will inherit the land. The secret of the LORD is for those who fear Him, and He will make them know His covenant.

**34:7,9:** The angel of the LORD encamps around those who fear Him. . . . For to those who fear Him, there is no want.

**103:13,17:** Just as a father has compassion on his children, so the LORD has compassion on those who fear Him. . . . But the lovingkindness of the LORD is from everlasting to everlasting on those who fear Him, and His righteousness to children's children.

**147:11:** The LORD favors those who fear Him, those who wait for His lovingkindness.

**Proverbs**
**10:27:** The fear of the LORD prolongs life.

**14:26:** In the fear of the LORD there is strong confidence, and his children will have refuge.

**16:6:** By the fear of the LORD one keeps away from evil.

**22:4:** The reward of humility and the fear of the LORD are riches, honor and life.

## DAILY READING
Read Proverbs 2:1–3:12. Mark the verse that stands out most to you today.

# DAY 3

## UNDERSTANDING DIVINE WISDOM

Both the Old and New Testaments tell us that earthly, human-centered wisdom will take us only so far; it will eventually lead us off track and will never help us lay hold of God. True wisdom guides us rightly because it is an expression of God's character—His righteousness, kindness, faithfulness, holiness, goodness, purity, mercy, grace, and love. Divine wisdom, then, is the only true wisdom.

When you hear the phrase "divine wisdom," what comes to mind?

### EARTHLY WISDOM

James gives us a helpful contrast between human-centered and divine wisdom. Read James 3:13-17.[11] Wisdom not from above is natural, earthly, and what?

James says earthly wisdom is demonic! It comes from the prince of this world who promotes shrewdness and manipulation. It's no surprise, therefore, that earthly wisdom would appeal to our fleshly appetites—to lust, greed, and pride.

Read John 8:44.[12] How is Satan described?

What is absent from Satan's nature?

Earthly wisdom is a delusion by the father of lies—a mastermind who traps us by our own sin nature and pride. Whatever is not from God is from the one whose character is completely devoid of truth.

### PRIDE AND HUMILITY

Pride is at the heart of our earthly nature because pride is at the heart of Satan's nature.

---

**[11] JAMES 3**

13-17 Who among you is wise and understanding? Let him show by his good behavior his deeds in the gentleness of wisdom. But if you have bitter jealousy and selfish ambition in your heart, do not be arrogant and so lie against the truth. This wisdom is not that which comes down from above, but is earthly, natural, demonic. For where jealousy and selfish ambition exist, there is disorder and every evil thing. But the wisdom from above is first pure, then peaceable, gentle, reasonable, full of mercy and good fruits, unwavering, without hypocrisy.

**[12] JOHN 8**

44 "You are of your father the devil, and you want to do the desires of your father. He was a murderer from the beginning, and does not stand in the truth, because there is no truth in him. Whenever he speaks a lie, he speaks from his own nature; for he is a liar, and the father of lies.

**[13] JOB 42**

5-6 I have heard of Thee by the hearing of the ear; but now my eye sees Thee; therefore I retract [maas], and I repent [nacham] in dust and ashes.

**[14] JEREMIAH 31**

19 For after I turned back [shub], I repented [nacham]; and after I was instructed, I smote on my thigh; I was ashamed, and also humiliated, because I bore the reproach of my youth.

Read Proverbs 3:7-8; 11:2; 15:33; and 16:5,18 from appendix A. What are the results of pride and what are the results of humility?

Can pride and humility coexist? Why, or why not?

Denying our guilt before a holy God is an act of pride—the most dangerous of all acts because it keeps us from humbly calling upon God and repenting of our sins. Sinfulness is not a popular topic, even among those who claim to embrace a Christian-oriented belief system. Many espouse a theology of the "goodness of man," even though it's disputed throughout Scripture.

To suppose that, through our own efforts, we can acquire those things that only God can provide is the height of folly, pride, and arrogance. The marvelous truth of Scripture is this: God intends for each of us to abandon our own efforts and to receive humbly His gift of eternal life, given by grace and received by faith in Jesus through the work of His Holy Spirit.[T6]

## DIVINE WISDOM AND REPENTANCE

Read James 3:13-17[11] again, noting the description of divine wisdom. As we've seen, wisdom from above begins with the fear of the Lord. We respond to the fear of the Lord in humility and repentance which leads to the knowledge of truth. But repentance, a work of the Spirit of God, is a term that is as richly used in Christian circles as it is poorly understood.

In the Old Testament, there are two concepts that are explicitly linked in the Hebrew understanding of repentance. The first concept is expressed in the word *nacham* which means "to be sorry, to mourn, to appease." The other concept is expressed in either *shub* meaning "to turn back, to return" or its synonym *maas* meaning "to retract, to cast off, to completely reject, to despise." *Nacham* is coupled with either *shub* or *mass* in certain contexts. Read Job 42:5-6[13] and Jeremiah 31:19.[14]

What caused Job to mourn and retract?

What caused Jeremiah's shame and humiliation?

**POINT OF INTEREST:[T6]**
WISDOM AND THE HOLY SPIRIT—In Acts 2:38 Peter said, "Repent . . . be baptized in the name of Jesus Christ for the forgiveness of your sins; and you shall receive the gift of the Holy Spirit." Paul tells us, "Walk by the Spirit, and you will not carry out the desire of the flesh" (Galatians 5:16). Furthermore, "the Spirit also helps our weakness; for we do not know how to pray as we should, but the Spirit Himself intercedes for us" (Romans 8:26).

God's divine wisdom is revealed through His Word and through His Spirit. The Spirit of God draws us into the secret places of God's heart and indwells the secret places of our hearts. The Spirit is simultaneously in touch with our weakness and with God's strength. He appeals to the Father on our behalf for our highest good, even when we don't know what we need. And the Spirit reveals to us the mind of Christ— the source of divine wisdom. Isaiah referred to the Holy Spirit and Christ, "And the Spirit of the LORD will rest on Him, the spirit of wisdom and understanding, the spirit of counsel and strength, the spirit of knowledge and of the fear of the LORD" (Isaiah 11:2).

*For further study:*
John 14:16-17
Acts 1:8,16
Romans 8:14,16
1 Corinthians 2:9-10
Galatians 5:22
Ephesians 1:13

**[15] MATTHEW 11**

21 "Woe to you, Chorazin!
Woe to you, Bethsaida! For if
the miracles had occurred in
Tyre and Sidon which occurred
in you, they would have
repented [metaneo] long ago in
sackcloth and ashes."

**[16] JEREMIAH 6**

26 O daughter of my people,
put on sackcloth and roll in
ashes; mourn as for an only
son, a lamentation most bitter.

**[17] COLOSSIANS 1**

16-17 For by Him all things
were created . . . all things have
been created by Him and for
Him. And He is before all
things, and in Him all things
hold together.

**[18] MATTHEW 13**

45-46 "Again, the kingdom
of heaven is like a merchant
seeking fine pearls, and upon
finding one pearl of great
value, he went and sold all that
he had, and bought it."

**[19] COLOSSIANS 2**

2-3 The wealth that comes
from . . . a true knowledge of
God's mystery, that is, Christ
Himself, in whom are hidden
all the treasures of wisdom and
knowledge.

In the New Testament, the Greek word for "repent"
is *metaneo*, meaning "to change one's mind and purpose."
*Metaneo* does not by itself carry the concept of mourning, but the link is obvious in various contexts. For
example, compare Matthew 11:21[15] with Jeremiah 6:26.[16]
What external symbols represent mourning, regret, and
grieving?

We see two things in the light of God's glory—His
majesty and our messed-up lives. Job repented in fear
when he saw God; Jeremiah repented in shame when he
saw himself. God's revelation of Himself causes a twofold
reaction in all humankind: fear (which turns us around)
and shame (which causes us to grieve our sin). If we're
basing our righteousness before God on our own per-
ceived goodness, then we haven't seen our wretchedness
and our desperate need for a savior. If we haven't
mourned in deep regret over our sins, then we have not
repented before God. And if we have not repented, we
have no basis by which to receive His wisdom.

**WISDOM IS A PERSON**

Proverbs describes wisdom using the imagery of a person—
a woman named Wisdom who existed before Creation.
Read Proverbs 8:1–9:10 from appendix A.

To whom does Wisdom call (8:4-5)?

How does Wisdom want people to respond (8:32-34)?

From these verses, we see that Wisdom calls to all
who will listen and heed her instruction—from the naive
to the scoffer (8:6,10,33). Those who respond to Wisdom will find treasures that exceed the value of anything
on earth.

Read Colossians 1:16-17.[17] How do these verses
relate to Proverbs 8:22-29?

Compare Proverbs 8:18-19 to Matthew 13:45-46[18]
and Colossians 2:2-3.[19] How do the New Testament
verses parallel the wisdom in Proverbs?

We see that Wisdom is more than literary imagery of a person. Wisdom is the Word that became flesh—expressed, fulfilled, and embodied in the pearl of great price, the hidden mystery, the only door to the kingdom of God—Jesus Christ.[T7]

## BRINGING IT HOME . . .

1. How often are the following attributes or traits evident in you? Rate yourself on each one using this scale: 0 = never; 1 = some of the time; 2 = most of the time; 3 = all of the time

__*arrogance*     __ gentleness  __ *jealousy*    __ purity
__unwavering  __ *disorder*    __ good fruits __ mercy
__reason        __ *falsehood*    __ hypocrisy  __ peace
__*selfish ambition*

   Ask God how you can grow in Christlikeness and diminish in the "traits of the flesh" (those in italics).

2. Which aspect of repentance (to be sorry and mourn over sin, or to turn back and reject sin) is most difficult for you? Why do you think this is true?

   - If the aspect of mourning is most difficult, review Proverbs 1:22-32 and 8:13. If you don't see sin as God does, what is the result?

   - If it is the aspect of turning back from sin, review Proverbs 3:1-8 and 8:32-36. What are the results of obedience?

3. Spend some time alone with God honestly expressing any difficulty you are having with repentance. He understands that sin entices because it appeals to our natural side. Ask Him to grow within you a hunger and thirst for the things that please Him.

**STUDY TECHNIQUE:**[T7]
TYPES AND SHADOWS—
Most events and characters in the Old Testament are best understood as physical or literal representations of what would become a spiritual reality in Christ. *Wisdom* in Proverbs, personified as a woman, is a picture or *type* that foreshadows Jesus.

## DAILY READING
Read Proverbs 3:13–4:13. Mark the verse that stands out most to you today.

## DAY 4

### EMBRACING THE WORD

How do you treat the things you treasure? Write your answer, then read Proverbs 2:1-11 and 3:1-4 in appendix A.

The father desires to share his store of wisdom, but he must first convince the son of wisdom's immeasurable worth. If the son will but hear and increase in learning, he too will come to treasure wisdom. The father knows that words have power. In fact, the words implanted in his son's heart and mind will wholly determine how he lives his life! If the son treasures wisdom, then the words of the father will become bound to him, written on his heart, adorning and gracing him (Proverbs 7:1-3).

#### HEARING THE WORD

In your readings you've probably noticed how often the Proverbs writer says, "listen," "hear," "incline your ear," "pay attention," "don't forget." Why do you think the writer repeated those phrases so often?

Wise words can be lost to competing messages—to distractions of life and demands of time. They can fail to sink in due to habits of denial, rationalization, and self-justification. It takes effort to really hear the Word of God, for hearing is more than just allowing sound bytes to pass through the auditory system. *Listening* is an action verb. Yet even good listening is not enough. Read John 8:47.[20] What does it take to have "ears that hear" the Word?

God's Word is revealed to us by His Spirit, which is given to us when we receive Christ as Savior and Lord. To *hear* God, then, we must be "of God." But in order to become "of God" (born again), we must be able to *hear* God. This seems like a paradox, doesn't it?

Romans 10:14-17[21] gives us insight. According to this passage, how does faith come? How does hearing come?

---

**[20] JOHN 8**

47 "He who is of God hears the words of God; for this reason you do not hear them, because you are not of God."

**[21] ROMANS 10**

14-17 How then shall they call upon Him in whom they have not believed? And how shall they believe in Him whom they have not heard? And how shall they hear without a preacher? . . . So faith comes from hearing, and hearing by the word of Christ.

**[22] ISAIAH 55**

10-11 For as the rain and the snow come down from heaven, and do not return there without watering the earth, and making it bear and sprout, and furnishing seed to the sower and bread to the eater; so shall My word be which goes forth from My mouth; it shall not return to Me empty, without accomplishing what I desire, and without succeeding in the matter for which I sent it.

Now read Isaiah 55:10-11.[22] Summarize what God says about His Word as it goes forth. Include the parallels of the impact of rain and snow on the earth to the impact of God's Word on our lives in the context of salvation.

God's power is resident in His Word, and the Word of God opens our heart to faith in Him. This Word-faith relationship reveals the importance of proclaiming God's words of life to a dying world. It also highlights the importance of studying the Word so that we are able to proclaim it accurately.

## UNDERSTANDING THE WORD

Read Proverbs 2:1-5 again (appendix A). After telling his son to receive, treasure, and pay attention to his words of wisdom, the father exhorts him to do what?

In these verses, the Hebrew word for "understanding" is *tebunah*, which denotes an act of wisdom or involves a faculty (for example, incline your *ear*, lift your *voice*, *walk* straight). *Tebunah,* translated "reasonings" in some contexts, involves both mental processing and physical response.[T8]

The corresponding Greek word for "understanding" is *sunemi,* which denotes collecting single features of an object and bringing them together (like a puzzle) into a whole; that is, putting it all together to make sense of it; to reason!

Understanding the Word requires that we search the Scriptures, meditate on the things of God, and subject everything we take in to both the full counsel of God (Scripture as a whole) and to sound reasoning.

## MEDITATING ON AND MEMORIZING THE WORD

Read Psalm 1:2[23] and Joshua 1:8.[24] "Meditate" in the Hebrew is *hagah*. It means "to moan, muse, or ponder." *Hagah* conveys an idea of wrestling with an issue or concept to achieve understanding and then receiving it deep into our hearts.

**POINT OF INTEREST:**[T8]
HUMAN INTELLECT AND THE WORD OF GOD—We cannot attain unto God through human intellect. Yet God is pleased when we, in submission and dependence upon the Holy Spirit, apply our reasoning abilities to understanding His Word. In fact, God's messengers gave the gospel, not as "pie in the sky," but by *reasoning* through the Scriptures.

Acts 17:1-3 tells us that "they came to Thessalonica, where there was a synagogue of the Jews. And according to Paul's custom, he went to them, and for three Sabbaths reasoned with them from the Scriptures, explaining and giving evidence that the Christ had to suffer and rise again from the dead, and saying, 'This Jesus whom I am proclaiming to you is the Christ.'"

God does not expect us to believe a nonsense message. Instead, He has given us a Word that will inspire, enlighten, and stimulate our thinking throughout our lives.

*For further study:*
Acts 17:10-12

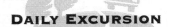
<sup>23</sup>**PSALM 1**

2 But his delight is in the law of the LORD, and in His law he meditates *[hagah]* day and night.

<sup>24</sup>**JOSHUA 1**

8 "This book of the law shall not depart from your mouth, but you shall meditate *[hagah]* on it day and night, so that you may be careful to do according to all that is written in it; for then you will make your way prosperous, and then you will have success."

<sup>25</sup>**JAMES 1**

21 Therefore putting aside all filthiness and all that remains of wickedness, in humility receive the word implanted *[emphutos]*, which is able to save your souls.

<sup>26</sup>**JOHN 1**

12 But as many as received Him, to them He gave the right to become children of God, even to those who believe *[pisteuo]* in His name.

<sup>27</sup>**JOHN 14**

15 "If you love Me, you will keep My commandments."

Compare Joshua 1:8[24] with the instructions from Proverbs 2:1, 3:1, and 7:1 (appendix A). What admonitions do you see in these verses concerning the Word?

The Word of God is to be kept and treasured. Do you treasure the Word? Does it have personal value to you? How is that value expressed in your life?

The true value of the Word of God is evident in its impact upon our lives. Do we read Scripture? Do we memorize it? Do we pray for insight? Do we seek to obey God's Word? If we aren't walking in wisdom, it may be because we aren't rightly receiving the Word into our lives.

Read James 1:21.[25] How *are* we to receive the Word?

The seeds of both wisdom and faith blow through the windows of hearing. When we hear and meditate on Scripture, we are implanting and cultivating the Word, thus hiding it in our hearts.[T9] Implanted (*emphutos*) comes from the root word *phuo,* which means "to bring forth; to produce." Just as surely as physical seeds planted in good soil will bring forth a harvest, so also will God's Word implanted in the heart bring forth spiritual fruit.

There are many benefits of meditating on God's Word. Read Proverbs 2:3-5,9-11, and 6:22-23. What are some of those benefits?

### BELIEVING AND OBEYING THE WORD

There's no direct reference to obedience in Proverbs 1–9, but the teaching is fully encompassed in the meaning of the Hebrew word for hear—*shama. Shama* (translated "to hear or heed") means "to continually listen *and* comprehend *and* obey." Obedience is an expected response to God's truth—a doctrine or teaching that is carried into the New Testament. Many times Jesus calls us to both *akouo*—"to hear and observe the facts objectively" and to *pisteuo*—"to believe in Him, both in intellectual assent and in confident trust."

Read John 1:12.[26] What right is given to those who receive Jesus and believe in His name?

The Greek word *pisteuo* in John 1:12 carries the concept beyond "believing about" or even "believing in" the Word of Christ. *Pisteuo* is a faith that takes us out of ourselves and puts us into Christ. This is a marvelous gift to those who have seen their own depravity before a Holy God. When we get a glimpse of the enormity of God's gift—that He has forgiven our sins and made us heirs of His kingdom—we are overwhelmed so that our love for God affects our thoughts, emotions, and actions. What is the natural outflow of that love, according to John 14:15?[27]

We've come full circle. Obedience is not so much something we do, but rather how we respond to the fear of the Lord and the power of God's love. When faith is fully persuaded, its behavior is consistent with that belief. If we don't desire to obey God's Word, then we should honestly examine ourselves in light of His truths. Do we really know Him?

## BRINGING IT HOME . . .

1. Take a few moments to further reflect on your personal value of God's Word. Answer honestly: How often do I read the Bible? Do I know how to study it? Do I value an education in God's Word as much as I do academic pursuits? Do I expend the same time and effort? Write one long-term goal for your biblical education. What will you do today to make progress toward that goal?

2. Meditate on the verses referenced in today's study and select one that seems to speak directly to you about God or about yourself. What change should the truth of this verse bring about in your life? Make this verse a personal prayer.

## STUDY TECHNIQUE:[T9]

TIPS FOR SCRIPTURE MEMORIZATION—It is important to deliberately memo-rize God's Word so that we're personally edified and equipped for His kingdom work. It isn't so difficult to commit verses to our short-term memory, but it is hard to retain them over time.

Try this technique for Scripture memorization: Write a verse (include book/chapter/ verse) on a three- by five-inch index card and put it on your desk, car dash, bathroom mirror, or refrigerator—wherever you will encounter it most often. Every time you pass it, read the card three times, until you can say that passage from memory before going to sleep and again before rising in the morning. Start a new card and repeat the process. Every week or two, read through the old cards so the Scriptures won't fade from memory!

## DAILY READING

Read Proverbs 4:14–6:19. Mark the verse that stands out most to you today.

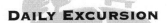

## DAY 5

### EXHORTING "MY SON"

**²⁸ 1 CORINTHIANS 15**

33 Do not be deceived: Bad company corrupts good morals.

**²⁹ EPHESIANS 4**

11-14 And He gave some as apostles, and some as prophets, and some as evangelists, and some as pastors and teachers, for the equipping of the saints for the work of service, to the building up of the body of Christ; until we all attain to the unity of the faith, and of the knowledge of the Son of God. . . . As a result, we are no longer to be children, tossed here and there by waves, and carried about by every wind of doctrine, by the trickery of men, by craftiness in deceitful scheming.

**³⁰ JOHN 17**

17 "Sanctify them in the truth; Thy word is truth."

**³¹ JOHN 16**

13 "But when He, the Spirit of truth, comes, He will guide you into all the truth; for He will not speak on His own initiative, but whatever He hears, He will speak; and He will disclose to you what is to come."

**³² REVELATION 21**

8 "But for the cowardly and unbelieving and abominable and murderers and immoral persons and sorcerers and idolaters and all liars, their part will be in the lake that burns with fire and brimstone, which is the second death."

In the first nine chapters of Proverbs, the father gives ten separate messages (oratories) exhorting the son to pursue wisdom. These exhortations, all beginning with "my son," are little pieces of instruction covering broad categories of life. Much of the father's teachings are actually warnings against developing relationships with people of ignoble character.[T10] Read the following verses from Proverbs and write the specific character types the son is told to avoid:

1:10-19

3:31

4:14-17

5:3-8

13:20

20:19

22:24

The son is admonished to evaluate the character of others and to avoid making companions of not only the criminal element but also people who are oppressive, gossips, quick-tempered, sensual, and foolish (*evilim*). How does Paul sum up these admonitions in 1 Corinthians 15:33?[28]

### THE BAIT OF DECEIVERS

The common denominator among the unacceptable companions from Proverbs is deception. Deception is an illusion created to intentionally lead others down a wrong path in order to gain some advantage over them. It is often remarkably effective, even on intelligent people, because it is usually laced with an element of truth and normally plays on another's personal weaknesses or blind spots.

What are some common uses of deception in our society today?

Read Proverbs 6:12-14 from appendix A and list some of the traits of the "model" deceiver.

Deceivers are treacherous. They can be found in all stations in life—from those with little influence to people of high regard, from blatantly evil people to religious imposters. Indeed, deceiving and being deceived are inherent in our humanity. The prophet Jeremiah wrote, "The heart is more deceitful than all else and is desperately sick; who can understand it?" (17:9). Yet deception has no place in the life of a Christian. Read Ephesians 4:11-14,[29] John 17:17,[30] and John 16:13.[31] What has God given to protect believers from being deceived?

- ▪
- ▪
- ▪

By maturing us in the knowledge of Himself and appointing us to be mutually accountable, God protects us from being tossed about by wrong doctrine and the trickery of others. Through His body of believers (the church), His Word, and His Spirit, we need not ever be deceived.

## GOD'S REACTION TO DECEIVERS

God is not pleased with deceivers. In fact, He hates—detests—deceptive ways. How does God promise to deal with the deceiver according to Proverbs 6:15?

Lying and deceiving others is a serious offense to God—one that will not go unpunished. Read Revelation 21:8.[32] What end will *all* unrepentant liars face?

Now read Proverbs 8:6-9. In contrast to the speech of deceivers, how is Wisdom's speech described?

**POINT OF INTEREST:[T10]**
BE *IN* BUT NOT *OF* THE WORLD —Let's be honest. When you hang around people, often they begin to imprint on you; they impact your thinking. A companion of fools soon suffers injury—that's reality. It is wise, therefore, for us to "hang" with people who have some wisdom.

This doesn't mean that we associate only with Christians. It does mean that in our associations with unbelievers we must be sufficiently different from them so that they will be either drawn to us or repelled by us because of our obedience to God's standard. No one ever remains neutral after encountering Jesus.

**[33] 2 Corinthians 6**

14-16  Do not be bound [heterozugeo] together with unbelievers; for what partnership have righteousness and lawlessness, or what fellowship has light with darkness? Or what harmony has Christ with Belial, or what has a believer in common with an unbeliever? Or what agreement has the temple of God with idols? For we are the temple of the living God; just as God said, "I WILL DWELL IN THEM AND WALK AMONG THEM; AND I WILL BE THEIR GOD, AND THEY SHALL BE MY PEOPLE."

**[34] Titus 3**

10-11  Reject a factious man after a first and second warning, knowing that such a man is perverted and is sinning, being self-condemned.

**[35] 2 Thessalonians 3**

14  And if anyone does not obey our instruction in this letter, take special note of that man and do not associate with him, so that he may be put to shame.

**[36] 1 Corinthians 5**

11-13  But . . . [do] not to associate with any so-called brother if he should be an immoral person, or covetous, or an idolater, or a reviler, or a drunkard, or a swindler—not even to eat with such a one. For what have I to do with judging outsiders? Do you not judge those who are within the church? But those who are outside, God judges. REMOVE THE WICKED MAN FROM AMONG YOURSELVES.

---

Deception is the antithesis of wisdom; therefore, deceiving cannot be a lifestyle of a true child of God. Those whose lives are characterized by deception and lying will be broken suddenly without remedy and will face eternal damnation.

### BEING SAFE AND BEING SALT

How can Christians avoid sinners (be safe) and yet win them to Christ (be salt)? The answer is to look at wisdom in the flesh. Jesus had a powerful impact on sinners. Because He remained dependent on the Father, Jesus didn't compromise His own morality when He interacted with them. And although Jesus was a friend of sinners, He never embraced them in His most intimate circles.

Read 2 Corinthians 6:14-16.[33] What restrictions are placed on relationships between believers and unbelievers?


To what specific types of involvement might these restrictions apply?


What danger is involved?


In the Greek, "bound" (heterozugeo) means "to be yoked up differently." Because we have no common value system, Christians must not be bound with unbelievers in any partnership, such as marriage or business. Although we must distance ourselves from their sin, Christians are never to disassociate or fail to receive the sinner. However, this is not true of so-called Christian brothers or sisters.

Read Titus 3:10-11,[34] 2 Thessalonians 3:14,[35] and 1 Corinthians 5:11-13.[36] How are Christians to treat those who profess faith in Christ yet blatantly and consistently live contrary to His commandments?


Proverbs 1–9 tells us that those who turn aside from wisdom, hate discipline, spurn correction, and refuse instruction will suffer social ruin, financial ruin, physical harm and, ultimately, death.[T11] On the other hand, those who embrace wisdom, insight, discretion, and discipline will be kept safe from temptations common to humankind.

Because of this promise, we should pay attention to Proverbs' description of the walk of a wise person.

## BRINGING IT HOME . . .

There are two important aspects to deception: keeping away from it as a personal way of life and avoiding others who make it their way of life.

1. If you are currently involved in any deceptive practices, bring them honestly to God. Tell Him exactly how you feel and ask Him for wisdom in how to eliminate deception from your life. Write down practical steps you can take, then ask a trusted Christian friend to pray for you and to hold you accountable in these areas.

2. If you are a Christian and in partnership with an unbeliever (whether in a dating, business, or other close relationship), make this relationship a matter of prayer. Honestly evaluate the impact it is having on your personal walk with Christ. In what ways is it pulling you away from Him? What changes do you need to make so that you are aligned with God's standards? If you are married to an unbeliever, pray for your spouse and seek to live an exemplary life that reflects Christ (1 Corinthians 7:10-15, Ephesians 5:15-21, and 1 Peter 3:1-2).

3. If deception has been (or still is) a way of life for you and you have never sought God's forgiveness, consider doing so right now. Turn to "God's Plan of Salvation" in appendix B for some help. Then share your decision with the leader of your study group, the pastor of a Christ-centered, Bible-believing church in your area, or someone who will be able to encourage the "new" you.

**POINT OF INTEREST:** [T11]

THE PERSONIFICATION OF WISDOM AND FOLLY—

The Proverbs father sums up his appeal by presenting Wisdom as a woman of excellence and Folly as a woman of ill repute. Folly embodies all the characteristics of the adulterous woman. Compare Proverbs 8:32–9:6 with Proverbs 9:13-18. Note the many contrasts between Wisdom and Folly; namely, light/darkness; open/hidden; pure/immoral; noble/base; holy/ungodly; true/false; faithful/disloyal; merciful/heartless; dependable/unreliable; giver/taker; honor/shame; love/hate; eternal/temporal; lasting/fleeting; other-centered/self-centered; invaluable/worthless; life/death.

Wisdom and Folly represent two philosophies, two value sys-tems, two ideas—one demonic, one divine—that are in constant rivalry. They both prepare a banquet; both bid all to come.

This dual invitation and the response of the wise and the foolish tie together the basic themes of Proverbs. Wisdom's banquet illustrates and points to Christ's invitation to us. Jesus offers us life and a relationship with Himself. He invites us to come like children, open-handed, to receive the bread of life.

## DAILY READING

Read Proverbs 6:12–7:27. Mark the verse that stands out most to you today. Because you read Proverbs 8:1–9:10 on day 3, you may want to mark a verse from this passage also. Review the verses you marked in each daily reading in unit 1 and select one to memorize. Use the suggestions in Side Tours T9, "Tips for Scripture Memorization," page 29.

*To the leader: Print "Fear of the Lord" vertically on the left edge of the board. You will use it during activity 2.*

1. In the book of Proverbs Solomon talks of four specific types of fools as shown below. Read Proverbs 1:7,20-22. For each type of fool give characteristics and modern-day examples. See day 1 of this unit.

   1:4 *Pethim* (simple)

   - Characteristics:

   - Modern-Day Examples:

   1:7   *Evilim* (fools)

   - Characteristics:

   - Modern-Day Examples:

   1:22 *Litsim* (fools)

   - Characteristics:

   - Modern-Day Examples:

   1:22 *Kesilim* (scoffers)

   - Characteristics:

   - Modern-Day Examples:

   At times even Christians display actions and attitudes that are associated with one of these four groups. Brainstorm ways to avoid or correct such actions or attitudes. Support your answers with Scripture.

2. The key verse of Proverbs tells us that knowledge begins with the fear of the Lord. What does this concept really mean? Name as many things as possible that strike fear of God or awe of His character in your heart. Do this in three minutes or less. Then divide into groups of no more than three and develop your own definition of the "Fear of the Lord."

Reconvene as one large group and have each group read and explain their definition.

3. Have volunteers read aloud the verses below. As each set is read, compare wisdom in the Old Testament to wisdom in the New Testament. What similarities are there? What do we learn about Christ from Proverbs?

   - Proverbs 1:20-22, 8:1-5 and John 7:37-38, 10:10

   - Proverbs 8:22-31; John 1:1,3,14; and Colossians 1:16-17

   In order to acquire wisdom, we must answer the call, humble ourselves, and receive what God offers. Our own pride can stop us from doing this. What are the characteristics of pride that make it so hard to come to Christ?

4. Read James 1:22. How does this verse compare to the admonitions given in Proverbs 1:2-3,8,33 and 2:1-5 (among many others)? How is it possible to hear and even give intellectual assent to a message and yet not act in accordance with that message?

   Share examples from your own life when you paid the cost of knowing what is right, but doing otherwise.

5. The first incidence of deception took place in the Garden of Eden shortly after Creation. Read Genesis 2:16-17 and 3:1-7. What is the progression from truth to deception? Why was Satan so successful in deceiving Eve? On what basis did he appeal to her (3:6)? If you were Eve's conscience, what could you have said to her to keep her from being deceived? If the book of Proverbs were available to Eve, what verses would have helped her?

Close by having each person read aloud a proverb he or she marked as being meaningful. Have each person share why this verse is special. Pray that the truth of that verse will be evident in that person's life.

# INTRODUCTION TO UNIT 2
## THE CHARACTER OF THE WISE, PART 1

*Destination: To examine Proverbs' characterization of the wise in terms of humility, righteousness, and teachability.*

As a guest at a luncheon meeting, I (Ken) found myself surrounded by men who would be considered "high ranking" among the citizens of Atlanta. Feeling intimidated and a bit out of place, I began trying to think of something to say that would elevate me in their eyes, something that would impress them. Because God is opposed to the proud, however, such a move would not have been wise.

We usually think of pride as a product of someone's inflated ego—of an exalted self-concept. Often, however, pride springs from our lack of confidence or low self-esteem. Regardless of its origin, pride is nevertheless a serious problem in our walk with God. God calls us to be humble in every situation and circumstance. That morning I had to remind myself that God had arranged for me to be among some of Atlanta's gatekeepers. My job as His ambassador was to stay focused on kingdom purposes—purposes that could never have been served from an attitude of pride.

In unit 1 we laid a foundation for understanding the wisdom topics presented in the book of Proverbs. In both units 2 and 3, we will examine the character of the wise. This unit will focus specifically on the traits of humility, righteousness, and teachability—each an antithesis of pride.

As you study, you will recognize that the best of people fall far short of God's wisdom in their thinking and behavior. Therefore, the character of wisdom as described in Proverbs will be convicting because it points to the character of Christ and to His righteousness.

Scripture's portrait of a person of noble character reveals our desperate need to be transformed, on an ongoing basis, by Christ Himself. We cannot develop Christlike character on our own, but we can grow in character through His Word and by the power of His Spirit. Your diligent study in Proverbs will prove invaluable in your development of godly character.

Living well is an art—a skill that wise men and women develop. The verses in Proverbs are tools for developing that skill, for *they are expressions of keen observations of life interpreted by divine insight.* They state probabilities of cause and effect yet leave room for exceptions—sometimes God-ordained exceptions! As we stated earlier, Proverbs are not promises but principles of life. As you study, may you heed Solomon's admonition, "The beginning of wisdom is: Acquire wisdom; and with all your acquiring, get understanding" (Proverbs 4:7).

## DAY 1

## THE WISE ARE HUMBLE

Humility is closely related to the fear of the Lord. Both are prerequisite to repentance and to receiving the knowledge of truth. What images come to mind when you think of humility? Is it a vice or a virtue, a curse or a blessing?

The seeds of humility are planted with our first insight into our helplessness and hopelessness apart from a Holy God. Humility takes root as we recognize that we can neither please nor appease the Almighty. But humility flowers only when we are broken.

Brokenness comes when we experience complete personal bankruptcy—relationally, emotionally, materially, or spiritually. None of us desires to to be broken. But brokenness has purpose. Read from Jesus' Sermon on the Mount in Matthew 5:3.[37] Who are the blessed? Why?

The Greek word for "poor" in Matthew 5 is not the typical working poor (*penichros*) but the *ptochos*—"those who crouch and cower; the beggarly." The *ptochos* are those who are totally without resources; they cannot help themselves. In Matthew 5:3, Jesus is effectively saying, "Those whose human spirit is broken, those who recognize their utter desperation before God are blessed!" Why? *Because poverty of spirit (that is, deep humility) is the point of entry into God's kingdom.*

Who are the blessed according to Matthew 5:4.[37] Why?

Mourning is the key indicator that we've seen our own depravity before God and realized that even our best deeds are tainted by "self." We've also grasped that we cannot be good enough—we cannot be *smart* enough—to lay hold of God. Mourning is not remorse (from being caught or being guilty), but godly sorrow and sickness over our sin. It is an expression of deep grief over having offended a pure and holy God. Humility and mourning are experiences that press us into God in desperate dependency.

---

**[37] MATTHEW 5**

3 "Blessed are the poor [*ptochos*] in spirit, for theirs is the kingdom of heaven.

4 "Blessed are those who mourn, for they shall be comforted."

**[38] JOB 5**

11 He sets on high those who are lowly, and those who mourn are lifted to safety.

**[39] ISAIAH 57**

15 For thus says the high and exalted One Who lives forever, whose name is Holy, "I dwell on a high and holy place, and also with the contrite and lowly of spirit in order to revive the spirit of the lowly and to revive the heart of the contrite."

**[40] LUKE 1**

51-52 He [God] has done mighty deeds with His arm; He has scattered those who were proud in the thoughts of their heart. He has brought down rulers from their thrones, and has exalted those who were humble.

**[41] DEUTERONOMY 8**

12-14 [Beware] lest, when you have eaten and are satisfied, and have built good houses and lived in them, and when . . . all that you have multiplies, then your heart becomes proud, and you forget the LORD your God who brought you out . . . of slavery.

**[42] HOSEA 13**

6 "And being satisfied, their heart became proud; therefore, they forgot Me."

Read Proverbs 15:33 and 18:12 from appendix A. What follows humility in each verse?

Read Job 5:11,[38] Isaiah 57:15,[39]and Luke 1:51-52.[40] What does God do for the lowly or humble?

When we come to God as humble, empty vessels, He fills us, defines us, and gives us true dignity.[T12] But humility is not natural. Human beings are far more comfortable with the enemy of humility, namely, pride.

## PRIDE

One way to understand humility is to look at its opposite. Read Proverbs 14:16 and 28:25 from appendix A, mentally noting the ways of the proud and arrogant.

The proud are quarrelsome, divisive, deceitful, and self-serving. Read Deuteronomy 8:12-14[41] and Hosea 13:6.[42] What condition makes us vulnerable to pride? Why?

Pride often manifests itself as arrogance. One of the Hebrew words for "arrogant" used in Proverbs is *rachab* meaning "to grow wide or large." Ease and satisfaction create a false sense of self-sufficiency and independence. Self-sufficiency is a seed of pride—a seed that Satan fully cultivates. Pride blinds us to our need for God. Instead of confessing, pride tempts us to boast in or cover up our sin.

Read Proverbs 28:13 and Psalm 32:3-5.[43] What is the result of concealed, unconfessed sin?

Compare Proverbs 28:13 and Matthew 5:4.[37] What does God offer those who confess, mourn, and forsake their sin?

Unconfessed sin injures our souls; confession and repentance set us free. An example is found in the life of

**POINT OF INTEREST:[T12]**
ON BEING HUMBLE—
Jesus says of Himself in Matthew 11:29, "I am gentle and humble in heart." He is the perfect example of a life of humility. Being God the Son, Jesus had all the right to glory, yet He humbled Himself to meet the needs of humankind. He could speak of His humility because He knew His own character.

For us, however, humility is elusive. As soon as we become aware of our humility, we are no longer humble. (You can't be humble and proud of it!) The same is true for righteousness and wisdom (those wise in their own eyes are fools). In our humanity, all our attributes cry out for recognition; but unlike Christ, our highest attributes are systematically destroyed by our own recognition of them. Self-focus, even in evaluating our "goodness," presents an occasion for sin. The answer is to focus on God's agenda and on the needs of others.

*For further study:*
Habakkuk 2:4
Zephaniah 2:3

[43] **PSALM 32**

3-5 When I kept silent about my sin, my body wasted away through my groaning all day long. For day and night Thy hand was heavy upon me; my vitality was drained away as with the fever heat of summer . . . I acknowledged my sin to Thee, and my iniquity I did not hide; I said, "I will confess my transgressions to the LORD"; and Thou didst forgive the guilt of my sin.

[44] **PSALM 51** *

3-4 For I know my transgressions, and my sin is ever before me. Against Thee, Thee only, I have sinned . . . so that Thou art justified . . . and blameless when Thou dost judge.
6,10-12 Behold, Thou dost desire truth in the innermost being, and in the hidden part Thou wilt make me know wisdom. . . . Create in me a clean heart, O God, and renew a steadfast spirit within me. Do not cast me away from Thy presence, and do not take Thy Holy Spirit from me. Restore to me the joy of Thy salvation, and sustain me with a willing spirit.
16-17 For Thou dost not delight in sacrifice, otherwise I would give it; Thou art not pleased with burnt offering. The sacrifices of God are a broken spirit; a broken and a contrite heart, O God, Thou wilt not despise.

* You may want to read all of Psalm 51 from your Bible.

David, king of Israel, who committed adultery with the wife of his loyal warrior, Uriah, and then arranged for him to be killed in battle. We read that Nathan the prophet confronted David, saying, "Why have you despised the word of the LORD by doing evil? . . . You have struck down Uriah . . . [and] have taken his wife" (2 Samuel 12:9). Faced with the truth, David was broken. He repented and mourned his sin. Read the excerpts from Psalm 51.[44]

Against whom had David really sinned?

What are God's sacrifices?

Rewrite the essence of David's prayer in your own words:

David basically confessed that there was no basis for forgiveness; he didn't deserve it. But with a humble and contrite heart, he repented of his pride and appealed to God's mercy and grace. God forgave David and restored him to a right relationship with Himself. Nevertheless, God did not leave the guilty unpunished. In 2 Samuel 12:10-14, God gave David a message:

"The sword shall never depart from your house. . . . Behold, I will raise up evil against you from your own household; I will even take your wives . . . and give them to your companion, and he shall lie with your wives in broad daylight. Indeed you did it secretly, but I will do this thing before all Israel. . . . Because by this deed you have given occasion to the enemies of the LORD to blaspheme, the child also that is born to you shall surely die."

David's humility restored him to a right relationship with God. But pride was costly. Read Proverbs 16:5, 18-19. How does God deal with pride according to these verses?

God judges and punishes pride, whether of kings or of paupers.[T13] And pride evokes disaster as humility evokes blessing. God is opposed to the proud but gives grace to the humble. We should humble ourselves, therefore, under the mighty hand of God, that He may exalt us at the proper time (1 Peter 5:5-6).

## BRINGING IT HOME . . .

1. Contrast being poor in spirit with having a sense of remorse.

2. Unconfessed sin is a powerful force that hinders our fellowship with God. Does your sin cause you to grieve? Do you confess it and repent? Do you then marvel at God's grace?

Find a quiet place where you can spend some undisturbed time before God. Ask Him to reveal any unconfessed sin. Ask Him to let you feel His grief, that you might release it to Him and then rejoice in His presence.

## HISTORY & CULTURE:[T13]

THE PENALTY OF PRIDE—
By warning and by example, God's Word assures us that pride will be dealt with surely and severely. Consider the warnings in the following Scriptures:

"No one who has a haughty look and an arrogant heart will I [God] endure" (Psalm 101:5).

"For the LORD of hosts will have a day of reckoning against everyone who is proud and lofty, and against everyone who is lifted up, that he may be abased" (Isaiah 2:12).

The Bible is filled with examples of the consequences of pride, and we would do well to pay attention—lest *we* fall. Read about God's response to the pride of kings in the following Scriptures:
2 Chronicles 26:8-21 (Uzziah)
2 Chronicles 32:9-21
  (Sennacherib)
2 Chronicles 32:22-26 (Hezekiah)
Daniel 4:28-37 (Nebuchadnezzar)
Daniel 5:1-30 (Belshazzar)
Acts 12:21-23 (Herod)

## DAILY READING
Read Proverbs 9:11–10:31. Mark the verse that stands out most to you today.

## DAY 2

### THE WISE ARE RIGHTEOUS

The book of Proverbs was written to give us wisdom—an internal attribute that begins with the fear of the Lord. The *goal* of wisdom, however, is not mental acuity but *righteousness*. What comes to mind when you hear the word "righteous"?

Righteousness is godly character. It is right living in right relationship with God as well as with others. We discern righteousness through the diligent pursuit of God's wisdom (Proverbs 2:1-11).

Two Hebrew words related to this concept are repeated throughout Proverbs. *Tsaddiq*, translated as "righteousness," means "blameless, innocent, just, right." *Yashar*, translated as "upright," means "straight, just, and right." These key words are synonyms and occur in Proverbs as many times as the words "wisdom" and "wise." Righteousness is implicit in every proverb. Indeed, it is the shoe leather of wisdom and the bedrock principle of Proverbs.

Over the next three days, we will be concentrating on verses that refer to the righteous. We'll be looking specifically at their thoughts and behaviors, their impact on others, and their blessings and rewards. Look up at least six of the following proverbs (more if you have time). Note what you learn about the character of the righteous, either by description or by contrast with the wicked.

|  | Righteous | Wicked |
|---|---|---|
| 11:3 | | |
| 11:23 | | |
| 12:5 | | |
| 12:10 | | |
| 13:5 | | |
| 15:28 | | |
| 21:26 | | |
| 24:16 | | |
| 28:1 | | |
| 29:7 | | |

---

**⁴⁵ROMANS 3**

10-12 As it is written, "THERE IS NONE RIGHTEOUS, NOT EVEN ONE; THERE IS NONE WHO UNDER-STANDS, THERE IS NONE WHO SEEKS FOR GOD; ALL HAVE TURNED ASIDE, TOGETHER THEY HAVE BECOME USELESS; THERE IS NONE WHO DOES GOOD, THERE IS NOT EVEN ONE."

**⁴⁶ROMANS 4**

3-6 For what does the Scripture say? "AND ABRAHAM BELIEVED GOD, AND IT WAS RECKONED TO HIM AS RIGHT-EOUSNESS." Now to the one who works, his wage is not reckoned as a favor, but as what is due. But to the one who does not work, but believes in Him who justifies the ungodly, his faith is reckoned as righteousness, just as David also speaks of the blessing upon the man to whom God reckons righteousness apart from works.

**⁴⁷GALATIANS 3**

11 Now that no one is justified by the Law before God is evident; for, "THE RIGHTEOUS MAN SHALL LIVE BY FAITH."

The Bible describes the righteous as people who *do* what is right, just, and fair. They are people of integrity who hate falsehood, wickedness, and injustice. The righteous are thoughtful, giving generously to the needy and being concerned for the rights and the life of the poor. The righteous are impartial in their judgments and speak out against wrong, defending the afflicted and rejoicing when justice and goodness prevail.

Many people of good character aspire to be righteous. The problem is that righteousness can neither be attained nor sustained by human effort.

Read Romans 3:10-12.[45] What is the state of every man and woman apart from God?

Isaiah 64:6 tells us that in our humanity, all our righteous deeds are like a filthy garment before a holy God. That's a pretty ugly picture. How, then, do we become righteous? How do we live righteous lives? Read Romans 4:3-6.[46] What verb is repeated three times in the verses from Romans that shows how we acquire righteousness?[T14]

Read Galatians 3:11.[47] How shall the righteous live?

Righteousness, according to Romans 4, is *reckoned* to us. "Reckoned" in both Hebrew (*chashah*) and Greek (*logizomai*) means "to account to, as a numerical value." This accounting term can be understood as an arbitrary crediting or assigning of a value to a person's account—whatever amount is needed to reconcile (zero out or cancel) his or her debt. Now, we've learned from Romans 3:10-12[45] that no one is righteous and that we all have a sin debt. God is just and cannot ignore our sin debt because it would violate His very character. "The LORD, the LORD God, [is] compassionate and gracious, slow to anger, and abounding in lovingkindness and truth; [He] keeps lovingkindness for thousands, [He] forgives iniquity, transgression, and sin; yet He will by no means leave the guilty unpunished . . ." (Exodus 34:6-7).

## LANGUAGE & LIT:[T14]

THE SIGNIFICANCE OF A VERB—Because of differences in tenses it is sometimes difficult to translate verb phrases from Greek to English. There is no English equivalent, for example, for the Greek perfect tense, which describes a past action with results that continue (and are continuing) into the present. Two examples of this perfect tense are found in John 19:28-30 (shown in bold below).

After this, Jesus, knowing that all things **had already been accomplished**, in order that the Scripture might be fulfilled, said, "I am thirsty." A jar full of sour wine was standing there; so they put a sponge full of the sour wine upon a branch of hyssop, and brought it up to His mouth. When Jesus therefore had received the sour wine, He said, "**It is finished!**" And He bowed His head, and gave up His spirit.

Why is this important? Thoughtfully read the following Scriptures:

"Inherit the kingdom prepared for you from the foundation of the world" (Mat-thew 25:34).

"He chose us in Him before the foundation of the world" (Ephesians 1:4).

"His works were finished from the foundation of the world" (Hebrews 4:3).

"The Lamb that was slain from the creation of the world" (Revelation 13:8, NIV).

What did Jesus mean by "It is finished"? At Calvary, God's pre-written history caught up with itself and continues reaching onward to the end of time!

**⁴⁸ JOHN 3**

16 "For God so loved the world, that He gave His only begotten Son, that whoever believes in Him should not perish, but have eternal life."

**⁴⁹ ROMANS 5**

8 But God demonstrates His own love toward us, in that while we were yet sinners, Christ died for us.

**⁵⁰ 2 CORINTHIANS 5**

21 He made Him [Jesus] who knew no sin to be sin on our behalf, that we might become the righteousness of God in Him.

**⁵¹ 1 CORINTHIANS 1**

30 But by His doing you are in Christ Jesus, who became to us wisdom from God, and righteousness and sanctification, and redemption.

**⁵² ROMANS 10**

10 For with the heart man believes, resulting in righteousness, and with the mouth he confesses, resulting in salvation.

By reason of His unchangable nature, God cannot leave our guilt unpunished. Sin carries a death penalty. This brings us to a truth so profound that we simply cannot comprehend it apart from revelation by His Spirit.

Prayerfully read John 3:16,[48] Romans 5:8,[49] 2 Corinthians 5:21,[50] and 1 Corinthians 1:30.[51] What stands out to you about the role of Jesus in these verses?

What affects you about the role of your sin in these verses?

Only in Christ's payment for our sin is God's absolute justice and absolute love reconciled!

- Nothing in our understanding can grasp why an all-knowing, all-powerful, all-sufficient, holy God would choose to love insignificant people.

- Nothing in our experience can explain why Jesus, God the Son, would willingly lay aside His power and glory to become imprisoned in a human body destined for a cross.

- Nothing in our rationale can conceive how God could give His only Son as a sacrificial lamb to satisfy the sin debt for all (from Adam to end times).

- And nothing in our human wisdom can perceive how, in Christ, God can grant us eternal life on the basis of the great exchange in 2 Corinthians 5:21.[50]

But God does. He credits the righteousness of Jesus to our bankrupt accounts. And when He does, true and sustained righteousness becomes increasingly visible in our lives as a testimony of His grace.[T14]

Read Romans 10:10.[52] How do we receive the salvation that is made available to us in Christ?

**BRINGING IT HOME . . .**

1. Review the two lists you created on page 40. Place a star by the traits of the righteous that God has already developed in your life. Circle those He is still working out in your life. Thank Him for His faithfulness to complete the work He has begun in you.

2. Ask God to reveal any of the behaviors listed under "wicked" that you need to yield to Him. Confess each one specifically and then spend time in prayer seeking His generous help in these areas.

3. Do you know anyone who needs to hear the message of God's ministry of reckoning and forgiveness? Begin praying for this person daily, asking God to reveal his or her need for forgiveness. Are you willing to be the one God chooses to use in bringing this person to Himself in faith?

**DAILY READING**
Read Proverbs 11:1-31. Mark the verse that stands out most to you today.

# DAY 3

## THE RIGHTEOUS MAKE AN IMPACT

**⁵³GENESIS 7 & 8**

7:1  Then the LORD said to Noah, "Enter the ark, you and all your household; for you alone I have seen to be righteous before Me in this time."

8:1  But God remembered Noah and all the beasts and all the cattle that were with him in the ark.

**⁵⁴HEBREWS 11**

7  By faith Noah, being warned by God about things not yet seen, in reverence prepared an ark for the salvation of his household, by which he condemned the world, and became an heir of the righteousness which is according to faith.

**⁵⁵GENESIS 18**

20,25-26  And the Lord said, "The outcry of Sodom and Gomorrah is indeed great, and their sin is exceedingly grave." . . . [Abraham said,] "Far be it from Thee to do such a thing, to slay the righteous with the wicked, so that the righteous and the wicked are treated alike. Far be it from Thee! Shall not the Judge of all the earth deal justly?" So the LORD said, "If I find in Sodom fifty righteous within the city, then I will spare the whole place on their account."

32  [Then Abraham] said, "Oh may the Lord not be angry, and I shall speak only this once; suppose ten are found there?" And He said, "I will not destroy it on account of the ten."

As Christians we receive the righteousness of God as reckoned or credited to us. God's righteousness affects the way we live, and the way we live affects the lives of those around us. Righteous people make a positive impact on others, beginning with their families and spilling over into their communities and their nations.

### THE IMPACT OF RIGHTEOUS BEHAVIOR

Look up the following Proverbs in appendix A to see how the behavior of the righteous impacts others. Then fill in the chart below. Write (F) if the benefit is primarily to the family, (C) if primarily to the community, and (F/C) if both. The first one is done for you.

|          | Righteous            | Wicked                        |
|----------|----------------------|-------------------------------|
| 10:21    | (F/C) lips fed many  | die for lack of understanding |
| 11:20-21 |                      |                               |
| 12:26    |                      |                               |
| 13:22    |                      |                               |
| 14:9     |                      |                               |
| 23:24    |                      |                               |
| 28:12    |                      |                               |
| 29:2     |                      |                               |

The righteous are a blessing to those around them and to those who come after them. Scripture's first mention of righteousness, in fact, concerns a man whose obedience affected the whole world.

Read Genesis 7:1, 8:1⁵³ and Hebrews 11:7.⁵⁴ Who was the *only* righteous person before God in that time?

Who and what were spared because of Noah's righteousness?

What did Noah inherit?

## THE IMPACT OF FAITH

The second mention of righteousness relates to the faith of Abraham (Genesis 15). Even with a barren wife and the handicap of old age, childless Abraham believed God's promise to make of him a great nation. God *reckoned* Abraham's belief as righteousness and He chose him "in order that he may command his children and his household after him to keep the way of the LORD by doing righteousness and justice" (Genesis 18:19). Like Noah, Abraham demonstrated his belief in God through his obedience.[T15] How do you think the faith of Abraham (the father of the Jewish nation) ultimately impacted the world?

Abraham's belief resulted in the birth of his son Isaac, and his grandson Jacob (whose name was later changed to Israel). To Israel was born twelve sons whose descendants became a nation—the one through whom the whole world was blessed with salvation in Jesus Christ.

## THE IMPACT OF PRAYER

Another example of the impact of the righteous is found in Genesis 18. Read Genesis 18:20,25-26,32.[55] According to this passage, what was about to happen to Sodom?

Abraham ultimately negotiated (interceded) with God to spare Sodom for the sake of whom?

We know that not even ten righteous people were found in Sodom because God completely destroyed that city. By the hand of angels, the Lord spared only Abraham's nephew Lot, along with his two daughters.

## THE IMPACT OF STANDING FIRM

These few biblical examples of the impact of righteousness on the lives of others barely scratch the surface of Scripture. Righteousness and its results are persistent themes throughout both the Old and New Testaments.

**HISTORY & CULTURE:[T15]**

RIGHTEOUSNESS PAST AND PRESENT—If the righteousness of God is only through faith in Jesus Christ, then what was the basis of the righteousness of Noah, Abraham, and Job who lived hundreds of years before Jesus died at Calvary? The answer is still *faith in Christ!* The Jews understood that Messiah (Savior) was coming to restore all things. That belief found expression in their God-ordained practice of substi-tutionary sacrifices of *the spotless lamb* as payment for their sins. In their obedience, they were looking forward *in faith* to the cross for their salvation—just as we, in faith, look back to it. The Jews never understood God's plan for the ages, but the faithful believed and obeyed God. Today, through Scripture, God's mystery has been revealed. His plan for the ages is now, and has always been, *you are saved by grace through faith in Christ.*

**⁵⁶PSALM 106**

23 [God] said that He would destroy them, had not Moses His chosen one stood in the breach [gap] before Him, to turn away His wrath from destroying them.

**⁵⁷EZEKIEL 22**

29-31 "The people of the land have practiced oppression and committed robbery, and they have wronged the poor and needy and have oppressed the sojourner without justice. And I searched for a man among them who should build up the wall and stand in the gap before Me for the land, that I should not destroy it; but I found no one. Thus I have poured out My indignation on them; I have consumed them with the fire of My wrath; their way I have brought upon their heads," declares the Lord GOD.

**⁵⁸1 SAMUEL 12**

24-25 Fear the LORD and serve Him in truth with all your heart; for consider what great things He has done for you. But if you still do wickedly, both you and your king shall be swept away.

God is looking for men like Abraham, men who will stand. "Stand" in the Hebrew is *amad*. It is translated "to take one's stand, to stand firm, to abide, to defend, to endure." Read Psalm 106:23[56] and Ezekiel 22:29-31.[57] How many righteous men did God seek to stand in the gap (or breach) for the land?[T16]

Do you ever feel powerless when you see the great wickedness in our land? God has not changed! He is still looking for a righteous man to stand in the gap for others. Scripture tells us that "the LORD is not restrained to save by many or by few"(1 Samuel 14:6). God's Word reveals many examples, in fact, where one righteous man stayed the hand of God's wrath by his faithful intercession. But can God's hand *always* be stayed? Read Ezekiel 14:13-14,16 below:

> "If a country sins against Me by committing unfaithfulness, and I stretch out My hand against it . . . even though these three men, Noah, Daniel, and Job were in its midst, by their own righteousness they could only deliver themselves," declares the Lord. . . . "They could not deliver either their sons or their daughters."

When a righteous man stands firm and intercedes, God hears; and He may relent of the calamity He has planned. But even if God does not relent, that righteous man has been obedient; and he can trust that even in judgment, God has ultimate good in mind.

### THE IMPACT OF LEADERSHIP

Let's take one more look at how the righteous affect the lives of others, this time focusing on leadership. Write what you learn from the Proverbs below:

|          | Righteous | Wicked |
|----------|-----------|--------|
| 11:10-11 |           |        |
| 14:34    |           |        |
| 16:12    |           |        |

If media-reported opinion polls are to be believed, most Americans are indifferent to the character of their

leaders. But God's Word says, "He who rules over men righteously, who rules in the fear of God, is as the light of the morning when the sun rises, a morning without clouds, when the tender grass springs out of the earth, through sunshine after rain" (2 Samuel 23:3-4).

Scripture tells us that character matters! Both history and experience confirm that righteous leaders have a profound effect on the overall health and well-being of a nation. Is it any wonder, then, that decades of governments without God have brought pervasive decline in the ethics and morals of our people? Read 1 Samuel 12:24-25.[58] What can a nation expect as a consequence for continuing immorality?

Could our country be in danger of being swept away in judgment? Are you indifferent or are you standing in the gap?

## BRINGING IT HOME . . .

It has been said that the true test of character is what you do when no one is looking or will find out.

1. Use these questions to test your character:

- Are there any secret sins (such as the worship of or longing for material things, prestige, power, or sex) in my life?

If you are a man:
- Have I taken seriously God's admonition to stand in the gap for my family? My church? My community? My nation?

If you are a woman:
- Am I faithful in prayer for my husband? Pastor? Spiritual and political leaders?

2. Use your answers to these questions as a means to determine how you personally need to stand in the gap. Bring these requests to the Lord.

## LANGUAGE & LIT:[T16]

MEN MUST STAND IN THE GAP— In this study, references to "man" always mean "humankind," unless specified otherwise. The Scripture in Ezekiel 22 is one of those exceptions. The common Hebrew word for humankind is *Adam*. The Hebrew word used in Ezekiel 22, however, is *ish*. *Ish* specifies male gender.

Women are certainly called to pray. But God has called men as warriors with specific duties to defend, protect, pray for, and stand in the gap for their families, their churches, their communities, and their nation. This Ezekiel 22 directive was the scriptural force behind the Promise Keepers "Stand in the Gap" Solemn Assembly that drew an estimated one million men to Washington, D.C., in October of 1997.

*For further study:*
Exodus 32:1-14
2 Samuel 24:10-25
Job 1:1-5, 42:1-9
Daniel 9:1-19

## DAILY READING

Read Proverbs 12:1-28. Mark the verse that stands out most to you today.

**[59] PSALM 37**

25 I have been young, and now I am old; yet I have not seen the righteous forsaken, or his descendants begging bread.

**[60] TITUS 3**

5 He saved us, not on the basis of deeds which we have done in righteousness, but according to His mercy, by the washing of regeneration and renewing by the Holy Spirit.

**[61] 1 JOHN 3**

7,10 Little children, let no one deceive you; the one who practices righteousness is righteous, just as He is righteous. . . . By this the children of God and the children of the devil are obvious: anyone who does not practice righteousness is not of God, nor the one who does not love his brother.

# DAY 4

## THE RIGHTEOUS ARE BLESSED

Not only do the righteous have tremendous impact on the lives of others, even to future generations, but they also receive personal blessings. Throughout Scripture the righteous are blessed and their lives are preserved through their righteousness.[T17]

Read Psalm 37:25.[59] What was David's lifelong observation of the righteous?

Over his lifetime, David had seen natural disasters, political upheaval, family heartaches, war, anarchy, and famine. Yet in his old age, David reflected positively on God's provisions for the righteous. Many of those blessings and provisions are spelled out in Proverbs. Read at least six of the following proverbs and note God's provisions for the righteous and the wicked.

| | Righteous | Wicked |
|---|---|---|
| 10:3 | | |
| 10:24 | | |
| 10:28 | | |
| 10:30 | | |
| 11:8 | | |
| 12:3 | | |
| 13:21 | | |
| 14:11 | | |
| 29:6 | | |

Physical and material provision, protection, deliverance, stability, steadfastness, hope, joy—so many blessings! Righteousness should be the deep desire of every believer. *Indeed, evidence of the righteousness of God is another hallmark of a true Christian.*

As we learned on day 2, God's righteousness is reckoned to our account when we accept Christ's payment for our sin debt, that is, salvation.

According to Titus 3:5,[60] what is *not* the basis of our salvation?

On what basis were we saved?

How did our salvation occur?

We are not saved because we are righteous—we are righteous because we are saved. Salvation is more than a spiritual makeover. By His mercy, we are reborn, regenerated, washed, and renewed by the Holy Spirit who gives us a hunger for righteousness. In Matthew 5:6 Jesus promised that those who hunger for righteousness will be satisfied. And God Himself will guide us in paths of righteousness for His namesake (Psalm 23:3).

Meditate on 1 John 3:7,10.[61] What do these verses say about the life of a believer?

If a person consistently does not reflect God's righteousness in his or her actions, what conclusion may be drawn about that person's relationship to God?

What about your life? Does it reflect God's righteousness? Are you growing in Christlikeness?

## THE RIGHTEOUS PLEASE GOD

By now you are seeing that wisdom, humility, and the righteousness of God are all woven into the life of the believer by the Holy Spirit. Note wisdom and the fruit of

## LANGUAGE & LIT:[T17]

BLESSED—The promise of blessing in Scripture is often misconstrued as referring to material wealth, good health, or worldly success. Indeed, Old Testament blessings often inferred reaping some tangible reward. Deuteronomy 28:1-14 is an excellent example of God's promise of physical blessings as a reward for Israel's obedience. However, the Old Testament is best understood as physical representations of what would become a spiritual reality in Christ.

The meaning of the word "blessed" varies. Some of the most common meanings of the verb "to bless" are "to set apart, to hallow or make holy (consecrate); to satisfy; to bestow good or grant favor to; to praise or glorify (to be spiritually joyful)."

Unlike the Old Testament, the New Testament references to being blessed move away from material blessings and present us with an interesting contrast to the world view. The Greek word for blessing, *makarios,* means "fully satisfied." But *makarios* is often found in seemingly paradoxical contexts. *Makarios* is sometimes translated "happy." However, happy comes from the English word "hap," which infers luck or favorable circumstances. *Makarios* transcends circumstances. Blessed is an abiding state of satisfaction that begins at the moment of salvation and increases with spiritual maturity (*Zodhiates Study Bible*, p. 11).

*For further study:*
Matthew 5:3-11; Luke 7:23, 11:28, 12:43; John 20:29; 1 Peter 3:14, 4:14; James 1:12,25, 5:11; Revelation 1:3

**62 2 TIMOTHY 3**

16 All Scripture is inspired by God and profitable for teaching, for reproof, for correction, for training in righteousness; that the man of God may be adequate, equipped for every good work.

**63 ROMANS 6**

16 Do you not know that . . . you are slaves of the one whom you obey, either of sin resulting in death, or of obedience resulting in righteousness?

19 For just as you presented your members as slaves to impurity and to lawlessness, resulting in further lawlessness, so now present your members as slaves to righteousness, resulting in sanctification.

**64 2 SAMUEL 22**

20-21 He also brought me forth into a broad place; He rescued me, because He delighted in me. The LORD has rewarded me according to my righteousness; according to the cleanness of my hands He has recompensed me.

**65 HEBREWS 12**

11 All discipline for the moment seems not to be joyful, but sorrowful; yet to those who have been trained by it, afterwards it yields the peaceful fruit of righteousness.

**66 ISAIAH 26**

9 At night my soul longs for Thee, indeed, my spirit within me seeks Thee diligently; for when the earth experiences Thy judgments the inhabitants of the world learn righteousness.

righteousness in James 3:17-18: "But the wisdom from above is first pure, then peaceable, gentle, reasonable, full of mercy and good fruits, unwavering, without hypocrisy. And the seed whose *fruit is righteousness* is sown in peace by those who make peace."

Read the following Scriptures. What "seed" do you see in these verses that can produce righteousness?

2 Timothy 3:16[62]

Romans 6:16,19[63]

Studying the Word and obeying God will increase the harvest of righteousness in our lives. Righteous men and women bring pleasure to God. And God rewards those who please Him.

Read 2 Samuel 22:20-21.[64] This is a song of David's after his men killed four of the descendents of the Philistine giant. What did God do for David? Why?

Read the following verses from Proverbs that contrast the fruits (in this life and beyond) of righteousness and wickedness. Write what you learn in the chart:

| | Righteous | Wicked |
|---|---|---|
| 10:16 | | |
| 10:25 | | |
| 11:18-19 | | |
| 11:30 | | |
| 12:12 | | |
| 14:32 | | |
| 15:9 | | |
| 18:10 | | |

What more could anyone want than intimacy with God, security in the Lord, productivity in His kingdom, and eternal life with Him! Would we pursue anything less? Yet Satan works diligently to disrupt the course of the righteous. As a result, even Christians can get sidetracked or begin to lose their appetites for righteousness.

Read Hebrews 12:11[65] and Isaiah 26:9.[66] What does God do, individually as well as corporately, to increase our appetite for the things that please Him?

God knows how to get our attention and turn us around; therefore, even when we are suffering His correction personally or experiencing the effects of His judgment as a nation, it is for our own good. God keeps us on the paths of righteousness, both as a blessing to us and for making us a blessing to others.

## BRINGING IT HOME . . .

1. List some of the tangible, physical blessings you are experiencing right now. Then thank God for each one.

2. Review the list of spiritual blessings from Proverbs that God gives to His people (page 48). Because these are gifts as a result of His grace, you have done nothing to deserve them. Write a prayer expressing your response to God.

## DAILY READING

Read Proverbs 13:1-25. Mark the verse that stands out most to you today.

## DAY 5

### THE WISE ARE TEACHABLE

**⁶⁷ROMANS 1**

18-20  For the wrath of God is revealed from heaven against all . . . men, who suppress the truth in unrighteousness, because that which is known about God is evident within them; for God made it evident to them. For since the creation of the world His invisible attributes, His eternal power and divine nature, have been clearly seen, being understood through what has been made, so that they are without excuse.

**⁶⁸ROMANS 1**

21-22,25-26,28  For even though they knew God, they did not honor Him as God, or give thanks; but they became futile in their speculations, and their foolish heart was darkened. Professing to be wise, they became fools. . . . For they exchanged the truth of God for a lie, and worshiped and served the creature rather than the Creator. . . .

For this reason God gave them over to degrading passions. . . .

And just as they did not see fit to acknowledge God any longer, God gave them over to a depraved mind, to do those things which are not proper.

In unit 1, day 2, we paid close attention to Proverbs 1:1-7,[1] looking specifically at the meanings of some key Hebrew words and phrases. We learned that the Hebrew word for "wisdom" (*chokmah*) related to gaining a skill; that "receive" (*laquach*) meant "to capture or seize"; and that "instruction" (*musar*) meant "to discipline, correct, admonish, reprove, or chastise." We also learned in Proverbs 1:3-5[1] that the wise would receive (seize) instruction (discipline), hear and increase in learning, and acquire wise council.

From these word meanings and Scriptures, we can conclude that *to be wise, one must remain wholly teachable, discerning truth by the power of the Holy Spirit.* In this excursion, we will explore the benefits of being teachable and the cost of refusing instruction.

The father in Proverbs 1–9 repeatedly calls his son to listen to his instruction and to gain understanding. The proverbs themselves admonish us to listen and learn.

In appendix A read Proverbs 26:12. What are we warned about in this verse?

Being teachable requires us to admit our own lack of knowledge and experience and to seek out others who can help us. Some of the strongest warnings against refusing counsel and being wise in one's own eyes are found in Proverbs 5. Read Proverbs 5:12-14,21-23. What can the "unteachable" expect in the end?

The folly of the unteachable will eventually be exposed. According to Proverbs, not being teachable is a primary characteristic of all those in the gallery of fools, particularly the *evilim* (those who actively oppose spiritual matters) and the *litsim* (scoffers—those who are arrogant and who hate God's rule). Our key verse, Proverbs 1:7,[4] says that fools *despise* wisdom and instruction. Why might the unwise be so afraid of truth and correction?

Read the following verses from Proverbs. Note what you learn about those who seek and accept godly instruction, discipline, reproof, or counsel as opposed to those who refuse it.[T18]

| | Accepts/Receives/Seeks | Refuses/Rejects |
|---|---|---|
| 3:11-12 | | |
| 9:8-9 | | |
| 10:17 | | |
| 13:1 | | |
| 13:18 | | |
| 15:31-32 | | |
| 29:1 | | |

The fool makes up his or her mind and then disregards evidence to the contrary. This person is the epitome of the attitude, "Don't confuse me with the facts." Protecting one's delusions, however, is costly. Without a teachable spirit, the fool cannot gain insight into truths about self, others, or the world at large. More importantly, an unteachable fool cannot gain insight into spiritual and moral truth, cannot learn from others, and cannot receive guidance from the Word. He or she will even reject the most obvious source of revelation God has given to all people.

Read Romans 1:18-20.[67] From what other sources may we learn wisdom and truth?

- 

- 

If we are wise, we can learn about human nature (including our own) by observing behavioral causes and effects. We also can learn of God from conscience and Creation, as well as His Word. But fools refuse to learn from *any* source. They deny or trivialize patterns of actions and outcome and offer authoritative opinions in areas far outside their realms of expertise. Being unaware of their own ignorance, fools glory in their self-deception. The arrogance of fools is often embarrassingly apparent to everyone but themselves, yet they reject even well-intended correction.[T18]

**POINT OF INTEREST:[T18]**

BLIND SPOTS—All of us have blind spots, and not just blind *spots* but whole regions where issues that are blatantly obvious to others are invisible to us.

People who are close to us, who love us, reveal those issues to us in a spirit that will help us grow. The Word tells us that the words of a friend are faithful and far more beneficial to us than the words of one who will flatter us with whatever we want to hear (Proverbs 27:6; 28:23).

If we refuse to hear truth from our friends or loved ones and continue on the same path, then we'll likely face the same issues again and again. Rebuke in the future, however, may come from those who don't love us and who are not so gentle.

No one, not even the wise, likes to be reproved or rebuked. Nevertheless, those who are wise will accept correction for the sake of the outcome. David said in Psalm 119:71, "It is good for me that I was afflicted, that I may learn Thy statutes." This is the attitude of the wise.

### [69] 1 SAMUEL 13

9-14 So Saul . . . offered the burnt offering. And it came about as soon as he finished . . . Samuel came; and Saul went out to meet him. . . . But Samuel said, "What have you done?" And Saul said, ". . . I forced myself and offered the burnt offering." And Samuel said to Saul, "You have acted foolishly; you have not kept the commandment of the LORD your God. . . . But now your kingdom shall not endure."

### [70] 1 SAMUEL 15

1,3,7,9 Then Samuel said to Saul ". . . Now go and strike Amalek and utterly destroy all that he has. . . . So Saul defeated the Amalekites. . . . But Saul and the people spared Agag [the king] and the best of the sheep, the oxen . . . and all that was good, and were not willing to destroy them utterly.

13-14,18-19 And Samuel came to Saul, and Saul said to him, ". . . I have carried out the command of the LORD." But Samuel said, "What then is this bleating of the sheep in my ears, and the lowing of the oxen which I hear?" . . . The LORD sent you on a mission, and said, 'Go and utterly destroy the sinners, the Amalekites. . . .' Why then did you not obey the voice of the LORD?"

20-23 Then Saul said to Samuel, ". . . the people took some of . . . the choicest of the things devoted to destruction, to sacrifice to the LORD your God at Gilgal. And Samuel said, ". . . Behold, to obey is better than sacrifice. . . . For rebellion is as the sin of divination, and insubordination is as iniquity and idolatry. Because you have rejected the word of the LORD, He has also rejected you from being king."

Even toward God, fools act presumptuously, rebelling against any commandment that reveals their folly or insufficiency. According to Proverbs 12:1, how does God view those who hate reproof?

Read Romans 1:21-22,25-26,28.[68] According to this passage what is the progression from truth (knowledge of God) to depraved thinking?

Read Proverbs 28:11. Foolish "know-it-alls" are found at every level of society, but the folly of the lofty is more visible and more apt to become historical record. In addition, the consequences of "high-level" foolishness are more extensive. Saul (Israel's first king) provides a classic example. Coming from humble beginnings, Saul had no claim to royalty beyond divine appointment. Once in power, however, he began to operate independently of God and ignore God's instructions through Samuel, the priest and prophet of Israel. Read 1 Samuel 13:9-14[69] and the excerpts from 1 Samuel 15[70] that highlight Saul's foolishness. List some of Saul's rebellious behaviors.

By offering a sacrifice, Saul knowingly violated the office of the priesthood. Later, Saul failed to obey God's command to completely destroy the Amalekites and all their animals because, in his own eyes, Saul was wiser than God. When challenged, Saul blamed the people. Saul finally confessed to protect his own image before the people, but he treated his sin as if it were trivial and did not repent of his rebellion before God. As a result, Saul not only lost the kingdom, he lost his mind (1 Samuel 8:10)! Unteachable Saul is remembered as a royal fool. How does Saul's end compare with the warning in Romans 1:21-22, 25-26,28?[68]

## BRINGING IT HOME . . .

1. Are there areas or issues in your life you need to change which those who love you have repeatedly pointed out? What are they? How do you respond when these areas are brought up—with defensiveness or a teachable spirit?

Bring these things to the Lord with an attitude of humility. Ask Him what you need to do to grow in these areas.

2. When you are faced with a financial or investment decision, whose counsel do you seek? What has been the outcome? Based on the outcome, should you stay with the same counselor(s) or seek new insight for future decisions?[T19]

3. Read Proverbs 1:20-33 and ask God to make you humble, teachable, and sensitive to the call of wisdom and to the claims of Christ over your life. Be quick to confess any time you refuse or act contrary to His will. Commit to staying in the Word often and long enough to guard your thoughts from your own "wisdom."

## POINT OF INTEREST:[T19]

GETTING BUSINESS COUNSEL—When we avoid reproof and accountability, we are prone to deceive ourselves. One place we are particularly vulnerable is investment decisions, especially when we're hoping to make a high return on our money. We become so convinced that our decisions are right that we refuse to hear objective opinion to the contrary. Instead of seeking spiritual and objective business counsel, we either avoid counsel altogether or seek out others who will tell us what we already believe and what we want to hear. Many times, advisors who are in enthusiastic agreement have a vested interest in the decision.

You don't have to go far to hear stories of great losses that could have been avoided if the investor had been willing to listen. Proverbs warns us that ruin is inevitable when we refuse to receive guidance, reproof, and discipline.

## DAILY READING

Read Proverbs 14:1-14. Mark the verse that stands out most to you today.

*To the leader: For this session you will use the board to list qualities of the righteous in activity 2.*

1. What are some common mistaken images that come to mind when the word "humility" is mentioned? Discuss where these misperceptions might have originated. Also discuss the difference between being humble and being weak.

   - As a group read Philippians 2:3-11. Based on this passage, how would you define humility? Jesus' life and death demonstrated the epitome of humility. Even though He is God, Jesus voluntarily humbled Himself to become a man. Even a brief look at His life makes it evident that humility   weakness.

   - Divide into three groups (one person can be a group). Have each group discuss one of the following passages and share how Jesus demonstrated both humility and strength. After several minutes, reconvene as one group and share your findings.

     John 2:13-22
     Luke 11:37-54
     John 8:2-11

2. Brainstorm and list on the board the qualities that should be evident in the person who is "in Christ." Be sure to include actions, attitudes, and attributes. Have two volunteers read Galatians 5:22-23 and 1 Corinthians 13:4-8.

   - What additional qualities, if any, are mentioned in these passages?

   - What "righteous" person has had the greatest impact for good in your life? What Christlike quality (or qualities) about this person made him or her so influential?

   - List some examples of the effects of the righteous in Scripture and in your personal life.

3. As believers, we should be influencing others for good through our actions and words, prayers, and example. Divide into groups of men and women.

   - Have the men discuss what it means to stand in the gap for their families, churches, communities, and nations (Ezekiel 22:30, Genesis 18:19). Also share

what they need from others in the body of Christ—both from women and other men—to encourage them to be leaders and to take a stand for Christ. As time allows, also discuss Titus 2:2,6-8 and 1 Timothy 4:12.

   - Have the women discuss what type of leadership they would like their husbands and the men in the church to take in each of these areas: spiritual, relational, and practical everyday living. Also discuss the role of older and younger women in the body of Christ. See Titus 2:3-5.

   - Reconvene as one group and share some of the key points concerning what men need from women and what women need from men as it relates to conduct, prayer, and leadership.

4. In His Sermon on the Mount, Jesus gave eight beatitudes, each beginning with the adjective "blessed" (Matthew 5:3-10). What does blessed mean? What doesn't it mean? Also read verses 11-12.

   - Would you agree or disagree with this definition of "being blessed"—seeing the goodness of God despite tough circumstances and being assured of better things to come in eternity with Him? Support your answer with Scripture.

5. Teachability is a mark of a maturing believer. In contrast, fools avoid all opportunities to learn.

   - Why do you think fools would rather remain in pride and self-deception than receive instruction?

   - If a Christian brother or sister (one you consider a close friend) has an area of self-deception or a moral blind spot, what steps would you take to help this person get back on the path of righteousness? What have you learned in this study that you would share with this person?

Close by having each person share the one proverb that has the most personal meaning so far. Pray that the truth of each proverb is lived out in the one who shared it.

# INTRODUCTION TO UNIT 3
## THE CHARACTER OF THE WISE, PART 2

*Destination: To examine the godly character traits of faithfulness, self-control, temperance, prudence, and diligence, and to learn the importance of seeking wise counselors.*

Many years ago, a man from the county road crew began to grade the old wagon road near the northeast edge of our family farm. My (Gail's) father ambled out to tell the road grader that he was on private property, but the man refused to stop. As calmly as he had gone out, my father returned and picked up his rifle.* My mother was mortified and we kids were stupefied as the grader was "notified" that he'd better be moving on. He did. My father could rightly be called strong-willed, but that description wouldn't tell the whole story. His was the first generation off the mountain, and my father's Scotch-Irish Appalachian value system remained well intact. In that subculture, an honorable man was compelled to protect the land, protect the family, and keep his word—no matter what. Far more valuable than personal achievement was strength of character.

Character is about personal boundaries. True character is revealed both by what a person does when nobody else is looking and by what he or she doesn't do, even if others approve. Scripture delineates many manifestations of bad character. Consider the following examples:

**1 Corinthians 6:9-10:** Do not be deceived; neither fornicators, nor idolaters, nor adulterers, nor effeminate, nor homosexuals, nor thieves, nor the covetous, nor drunkards, nor revilers, nor swindlers, shall inherit the kingdom of God.

**Ephesians 5:3-5:** But do not let immorality or any impurity or greed even be named among you . . . and there must be no filthiness and silly talk, or coarse jesting, which are not fitting. . . . No immoral or impure person . . . has an inheritance in the kingdom of Christ and God.

This list of offenses is sobering. Sin not only incurs God's wrath, but apart from Christ, it also keeps us from inheriting God's kingdom. In this short study, we cannot evaluate all the negatives that Scripture tells us to avoid. We can, however, concentrate on imitating the character of God. Godly character displaces sin; therefore, be encouraged by these Scriptures:

**Philippians 4:8-9:** Finally, brethren, whatever is true . . . honorable . . . right . . . pure . . . lovely . . . of good repute, if there is any excellence and if anything worthy of praise, let your mind dwell on these things. . . . Practice these things.

**Romans 12:2:** And do not be conformed to this world, but be transformed by the renewing of your mind, that you may prove what the will of God is, that which is good and acceptable and perfect.

Pursuing God and applying wisdom from His Word will produce the fruit of the Spirit in our lives—love, joy, peace, patience, kindness, goodness, faithfulness, gentleness, self-control, humility, righteousness, and truth (Galatians 5:22-23). As you work through this unit (part 2 in our study of character) ask God to increase the manifestations of godly character in your life.

*The family memory bank was unsure whether the rifle was used with the road grader or a man from the city planning commission. Both were men associated with the "intruding" government.

## DAY 1

## THE WISE ARE FAITHFUL

"A faithful man will abound with blessings" (Proverbs 28:20). What does it mean to be faithful? The various Hebrew words that are often transcribed "faithful" all come from the root word *aman* meaning "to confirm or support." *Aman* and its derivatives have been translated "honest, responsible, stable, trustworthy, truthful, enduring, established, and reliable." It's no surprise, then, that "faithful" is used most often in reference to God Himself.

Read Deuteronomy 7:9[71] and 32:4.[72] In what ways is God faithful according to these passages?

Because the wise emulate God's character, they will be faithful to Him. According to Deuteronomy 10:12-13,[73] what five things does the Lord require as an expression of our faithfulness to Him?

- ▪
- ▪
- ▪
- ▪
- ▪

For what purpose does He require these things?

Our Lord is a covenant-keeping God. He is just in *all* His interactions in our lives. The wise are faithful to Him—to His laws, to His standards of holiness, and to His creation. The wise know that God has their best interests at heart and that all His commandments are intended *for their own good.*

### FAITHFULNESS: GIVING OUR WHOLE HEARTS

In Proverbs 23:26, God tells us, "Give me your heart . . . and let your eyes delight in my ways." In practice, our whole spiritual life could be reduced to this proverb; for when God has our whole heart and we desire what He

---

**Sidebar references:**

[71] **DEUTERONOMY 7**
9 Know therefore that the LORD your God, He is God, the faithful God, who keeps His covenant and His lovingkindness to a thousandth generation with those who love Him and keep His commandments.

[72] **DEUTERONOMY 32**
4 The Rock! His work is perfect, for all His ways are just; a God of faithfulness and without injustice, righteous and upright is He.

[73] **DEUTERONOMY 10**
12-13 What does the LORD your God require from you, but to fear the LORD your God, to walk in all His ways and love Him, and to serve the LORD your God with all your heart and with all your soul, and to keep the LORD's commandments . . . for your good?

[74] **ISAIAH 55**
9 "For as the heavens are higher than the earth, so are My ways higher than your ways, and My thoughts than your thoughts."

[75] **ROMANS 11**
33 Oh, the depth of the riches both of the wisdom and knowledge of God! How unsearchable are His judgments and unfathomable His ways!

[76] **JOB 7**
17 What is man that Thou dost magnify him, and that Thou art concerned about him?

desires, everything else falls into its proper perspective. Our human tendency, however, is to yield only portions of our heart and life to Him. The truth is, we really don't trust that He knows (or perhaps cares about) what's best for us or what's for "our good." At the center of our doubt is a failure to comprehend an earnest measure of God's love. That is, we don't trust God because we cannot grasp how the *All-Sufficient* could really love and want a personal relationship with the *insignificant*.

Read Isaiah 55:9[74] and Romans 11:33.[75] Why can't we understand God's love more fully?

Compared to God, we know nothing! His thinking so vastly exceeds ours that it's ridiculous to compare the two. God knows all about us—our lives, the lives of those around us, our past, and our future. We cannot explain His ways because they transcend *everything* in our human experience. This is especially true of His unconditional love.

Read Job 7:17[76] and Psalm 8:3-5.[77] What is the fundamental question with which both Job and David wrestled? Restate their question in your own words.

Job and David never really unraveled the mystery that so intrigued them, but they accepted God's Word as truth. Our faithfulness to God also will rest in accepting what God says about Himself—that He is sovereign, that He created us, that He loves us, and that He desires to crown us with glory *simply on the basis of His ways!*

### EXPRESSIONS OF FAITH

God's farsighted choices for our highest good will often contradict our nearsighted inclinations and desires.[T20] How we respond in these stressful times will reveal the truth about our faith and trust in God.

We express our faithfulness to God as we agree that everything He says is important and everything He does is right. We expand our faithfulness as we respond to His call, even when things seem to be pointing in the wrong direction. We experience His faithfulness when we examine the cumulative results of events in our lives

**POINT OF INTEREST:**[T20]
FAITHFUL FRIEND OR ENABLER?—My (Ken's) desire in ministry is to lead people to the Source of truth so that they are able to act intelligently. Christians need to learn to work through their emotions and to think things through in relation to God's commandments before they respond.

Action based solely on emotion is dangerous. One place we can see this danger is in families where one member has an addiction or a destructive habit, such as anger. Often our emotional reaction is to enable (to rescue or run interference for) that spouse, child, or parent. This response, however, makes the enabler part of the problem. For example, Solomon wrote in Proverbs 19:19, "A man of great anger shall bear the penalty; for if you rescue him, you will only have to do it again." From outbursts of anger to alcoholism, wisdom calls for allowing our loved ones to suffer the consequences of their behavior so that their destructive patterns might be broken. Being an enabler is *not* being a faithful spouse or friend. Faithfulness is expressed in suffering with (not for) those you love in order to achieve their highest good.

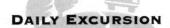
**78 HOSEA 4**

1 Listen to the word of the LORD, O sons of Israel, for the LORD has a case against the inhabitants of the land, because there is no faithfulness or kindness or knowledge of God in the land.

**77 PSALM 8**

3-5 When I consider Thy heavens, the work of Thy fingers, the moon and the stars, which Thou hast ordained; what is man, that Thou dost take thought of him? And the son of man, that Thou dost care for him? Yet Thou hast made him a little lower than God, and dost crown him with glory and majesty!

and marvel at the superiority of the long-range outcomes when we've followed His ways. The faithful will abound in blessings. But what of the unfaithful? Read Hosea 4:1.[78] What three things are lacking in the land that cause the Lord to judge its inhabitants?

- 
- 
- 

Which of these three is weakest in your life?

It is no coincidence that the lack of faithfulness in this passage is coupled with a lack of knowledge of God. Without understanding who God is and how He wants us to live, we cannot be faithful. These two concepts are defined only in God's Word. Being faithful, therefore, requires concentrating on and abiding in God's Word and making sure that His Word abides in us.

**THE CHARACTER OF THE FAITHFUL**

Read the following verses from Proverbs (see appendix A) and write below what you learn about the character of the faithful and the results of being faithful:

14:5

25:13

27:6

28:20

The faithful are honest, refreshingly dependable, and truthful, even when the truth hurts (Proverbs 27:6). They are righteous, fruit-bearing, full of integrity, and trusting; therefore, the faithful have a unique freedom to rest in God, knowing that every life experience will have eternal value. In addition to being faithful to God, the wise are faithful to others. Ask God to increase your faithfulness as well as your faith in Him.

**BRINGING IT HOME . . .**

1. List the attributes of God that encourage and increase your faith in Him.

2. Take time to do some spiritual spring cleaning. Ask God if He has your whole heart. Use these questions to help you evaluate yourself:

   - Would I feel uncomfortable with any of my habits if everyone in the room knew about them?

   - If all of my thoughts were revealed to those around me, would they embarrass me or my family?

   - Do I have any desires or dreams that I am afraid to discuss with other Christians, much less with God?

   Based on God's answer (as revealed through conviction), release any areas of your life He brings to mind. If it's an area you don't want to release, be honest about it to God. Ask Him to plant His desires in your heart.

**DAILY READING**
Read Proverbs 14-35. Mark the verse that stands out most to you today.

## DAY 2

## DAY 2

### THE WISE ARE SELF-CONTROLLED

Proverbs 25:28 gives us a wonderful word picture for understanding the importance of self-control: "Like a city that is broken into and without walls is a man who has no control over his spirit." Controlling our human spirit means bringing our emotional, material, and physical desires under subjection to our will. Being self-controlled is not about denying our human desires; it's about not being enslaved to them.

Read the Proverbs listed below and write down what you learn about the self-controlled:

10:19

14:16

16:32

17:27

29:11

### CONTROLLED BY OUR PAST?

Self-control presupposes a knowledge of right and wrong as well as a proper sense of guilt and shame. Unfortunately, these concepts have been all but lost in our culture. When someone exhibits highly ethical behavior or self-restraint, it literally makes the news![T21] Blaming others for our lack of self-control is so pervasive, on the other hand, that even the Christian community has largely bought into it.

Many Christians quote Deuteronomy 5:9[79] as evidence that people cannot help being "the way they are" because of poor parenting or early life traumas. Read Deuteronomy 5:9.[79] Who is speaking?

For whose sins might the children be punished?

Let's put this passage in context. Moses is standing before the people of Israel, repeating the giving of the Law and quoting God's description of Himself. Alone, this passage may appear to suggest that indeed, God charges a man's sin to his children's (and grandchildren's) accounts. But does this interpretation fit with the whole counsel of God?

---

### [79] DEUTERONOMY 5

9 "You shall not worship [other gods] or serve them; for I, the LORD your God, am a jealous God, visiting the iniquity of the fathers on the children, and on the third and the fourth generations of those who hate Me."

### [80] EZEKIEL 18

2-5,7-9 What do you mean by using this proverb . . . 'The fathers eat the sour grapes, but the children's teeth are set on edge'? "As I live," declares the Lord GOD, "you are surely not going to use this proverb in Israel anymore. Behold, all souls are Mine; the soul of the father as well as the soul of the son is Mine. The soul who sins will die. But if a man is righteous, and practices justice and righteousness . . . [and] does not oppress anyone, but restores to the debtor his pledge, does not commit robbery, but gives his bread to the hungry, and covers the naked with clothing, if he does not lend money on interest . . . if he keeps his hand from iniquity, and executes true justice . . .walks in My statutes and My ordinances so as to deal faithfully—he is righteous and will surely live," declares the Lord GOD.

### [81] ROMANS 6

12-14 Therefore do not let sin reign in your mortal body that you should obey its lusts, and do not go on presenting the members of your body to sin as instruments of unrighteousness; but present yourselves to God as those alive from the dead, and your members as instruments of righteousness to God. For sin shall not be master over you, for you are not under law, but under grace.

Read Ezekiel 18:2-5,7-9.[80] Who is speaking in this passage?

For whose sin is each person accountable?

At Creation, God set forth equally binding laws—physical laws to govern the earth and spiritual laws to govern people. We know that defying physical laws brings about natural consequences, some immediate and some residual. Gravity, for example, will prevail over the person who steps off a ten-story building. Likewise, defying God's spiritual laws will bring about spiritual consequences, some immediate and some *residual*.

Read Deuteronomy 5:9 again. For whom should the people have been concerned?

Moses is reminding the people of the residual consequences of sin; that is, the series of cause-and-effect circumstances that sin sets in motion. Moses is admonishing the people to live righteously—for the sake of future generations as well as for the immediate one. If you'll read the "sour grapes" proverb carefully, however, you'll find that it's essentially an about-face of the Deuteronomy 5:9 principle. This proverb in Ezekiel traded post-generational responsibility (as God directed through Moses) for pre-generational blame. Sound familiar?

God, however, makes personal accountability abundantly clear in Ezekiel 18. The "sour grapes" proverb (which is *not* in the book of Proverbs) wasn't just untrue, it was heresy. Even under the Law, God didn't want to hear it!

According to Romans 6:12-14,[81] what does *not* master us?

Why?

If Scripture is true (and it is), then we are without excuse. In Christ, sin is not our master, no matter what

## POINT OF INTEREST:[T21]

ON TAKING RESPONSIBILITY— When a mother learned of her son's participation in a recent convenience store robbery, she loaded him in her car, drove him down to the police station, and turned him in. Robberies are commonplace. This robbery didn't make national news. What *was* newsworthy, however, was that this single mom had made her under-age son take responsibility for his action.

What was once the culturally accepted "right thing to do" has become an anomaly. Far more typical today are the parents who accuse authorities of mistreating their child, even when he or she has been caught red-handed!

If we expect our children to be responsible, then we must begin to hold them accountable for their wrong deeds at an early age. Kids should experience the full force of the consequences of their behavior while parents have the power to keep those consequences within safe limits.

**[82] NUMBERS 5**

6-7 "Speak to the sons of Israel, 'When a man or woman commits any of the sins of mankind, acting unfaithfully against the LORD, and that person is guilty, then he shall confess his sins which he has committed, and he shall make restitution in full for his wrong, and add to it one-fifth of it, and give it to him whom he has wronged.'"

**[83] 1 JOHN 1 & 2**

1:9-10 If we confess our sins, He is faithful and righteous to forgive us our sins and to cleanse us from all unrighteousness. If we say that we have not sinned, we make Him a liar, and His word is not in us.

2:1-3 My little children, I am writing these things to you that you may not sin. And if anyone sins, we have an Advocate with the Father, Jesus Christ the righteous; and He Himself is the propitiation for our sins; and not for ours only, but also for those of the whole world. And by this we know that we have come to know Him, if we keep His commandments.

kinds of family circumstances we may have inherited. The lives of our forefathers may be responsible for some of our personal (or national) circumstances—but they are not responsible for our personal sin. As Paul stated in 1 Corinthians 10:13, "God is faithful, who will not allow you to be tempted beyond what you are able, but with the temptation will provide the way of escape also, that you may be able to endure it."

God's remedy for sin is not excuse. Read Numbers 5:6-7[82] and 1 John 1:9-10, 2:1-3.[83] When we've sinned, what must we do to be restored?

Whether under the Old Testament Law or under New Testament grace in Christ, God tells us not to excuse our sin. Rather we are to confess, repent, and wherever possible, make restitution. Our sin debt has already been paid in full by Jesus Christ, our advocate. When we confess and repent, God is moved to apply Christ's payment to our account that we may be restored to fellowship with Him.

### SELF-CONTROLLED VS. SPIRIT-CONTROLLED

We don't have to be Christians to achieve a level of self-control. Most children can be trained to act, or to not react, with a good balance of:

- Accountability (principle of cause and effect),
- Discipline (sufficiently negative consequences and new instruction), and
- Rewards (reinforcement of desired behavior).

Read Proverbs 22:6 and 29:15. What are the results of discipline and the lack of discipline?

A self-controlled adult is usually an off-spring of self-disciplined (and child-disciplining) parents—who may or may not know God.[T22] While discipline and modeling is an effective way to teach children to control their behavior, the process will not automatically adjust a child's internal responses to frustrations, anxieties, and anger. Kids need to develop a tranquil spirit—and so do we!

Read Proverbs 14:30. What is the benefit of a tranquil heart?

What is the product of passion?

As long as we live in a fallen world, we will be frustrated by temptations and by people who rankle us. External frustration leads to internal turmoil; and we must contend with our emotions. Otherwise, our pent-up emotions will destroy our bodies as well as increase the likelihood that we'll eventually vent in inappropriate ways.

Though a good thing, "self" control generally affects only external behavior. It's human decency. But internal grace and peace that surpasses all understanding is ours only by the work of the Spirit. The fruit of the Spirit that is called "self-control," therefore, is really "Spirit-control." It is decent to behave with dignity and restraint but divine to release our anger and forgive our offenders. It is decent to subject our desires to our will but divine to submit our desires to His will. Being Spirit-controlled goes beyond human will, for it works on the *heart* of the matter.

**BRINGING IT HOME . . .**

1. Are there any specific weaknesses or sin patterns in your family background? If so, what are you doing (or can you do) to assure they stop with you? (It is sometimes prudent to seek the help of a Christian counselor or pastor to help you experience freedom.)

2. In what ways did your parents contribute to your being self-controlled? Thank them for their positive input.

3. What have you learned about this area that you want to pass on to your children (whether by physical or spiritual birth)?

**POINT OF INTEREST:**[T22]

ON BEING SELF-CONTROLLED—When I (Ken) was a kid, I liked the smell of gasoline. I would pump the gas and try to get my nose close enough to smell the fumes. Then one day, I really got a whiff (actually a sniff) of gas—I thought I was going to die! That ended my smelling of gas fumes. Still, I continued doing other things to excess, such as actually eating until I was sick!

Perhaps someone should have taught me Proverbs 25:16, "Have you found honey? Eat only what you need, lest you have it in excess and vomit it."

Proverbs has much to say about self-control, from simple overeating to controlling our sexual appetites. You may find the following Proverbs helpful:
**Alcohol:** Proverbs 23:29-35
**Eating:** 23:1-3,19-21
**Finances:** 23:4-5
**Contentment:** 27:20

**DAILY READING**
Read Proverbs 15:1-33. Mark the verse that stands out most to you today.

## DAY 3

### THE WISE ARE PEACEABLE

There is a lot of misinformation about anger and the Christian. One extreme is the belief that Christians should never express or even feel anger. The other extreme is the attitude that anger is a natural human reaction; therefore, we are not responsible for it. What does God's Word say? Read the following proverbs and write what you learn about the slow anger of the wise.

**Anger of the Wise**

14:29

15:18

16:32

19:11

Proverbs tells us that the wise have great understanding and the ability to quell trouble and overlook offenses. They freely give grace and forgiveness. In short, they have long fuses. Their self-control makes them better than the mighty.

Now look up the following proverbs to discover God's view of the fool's anger. Write down your findings.

**Anger of the Foolish**

14:29

15:18

19:19

29:22

Proverbs says that the hot-tempered person is a fool to be avoided because he or she angers quickly, speaks harshly, stirs up strife, and abounds in transgressions.

While both the wise and the foolish experience or feel anger, what they do with it differs, in frequency, degree, expression (or response), and motive.

Read Psalm 86:15[84] and Deuteronomy 32:21.[85] Who in these verses was "slow to anger" yet eventually became provoked?

---

[84]**PSALM 86**

15 But Thou, O Lord, art a God merciful and gracious, slow to anger and abundant in lovingkindness and truth.

[85]**DEUTERONOMY 32**

21 "They have made Me jealous with what is not God; they have provoked Me to anger with their idols. So I will make them jealous with those who are not a people; I will provoke them to anger with a foolish nation."

[86]**EPHESIANS 4**

26-27 BE ANGRY [orge], AND YET DO NOT SIN; do not let the sun go down on your anger, and do not give the devil an opportunity.

[87]**JAMES 1**

19-20 This you know, my beloved brethren. But let everyone be quick to hear, slow to speak and slow to anger [orge]; for the anger of man does not achieve the righteousness of God.

[88]**EPHESIANS 4**

31 Let all bitterness and wrath [thumos] and anger [orge] and clamor and slander be put away from you, along with all malice.

[89]**COLOSSIANS 3**

8-10 But now you also, put them all aside: anger, wrath, malice, slander, and abusive speech from your mouth . . . since you laid aside the old self with its evil practices, and have put on the new self who is being renewed to a true knowledge according to the image of the One who created him.

Many times in Scripture, God described Himself as "slow to anger." Nevertheless, rebellious Israel eventually provoked His wrath. Is the Old Testament view of anger consistent with New Testament teaching on anger and Christian living? Read Ephesians 4:26-27[86] and James 1:19-20.[87] What are the instructions to Christians regarding anger?

What does our anger fail to achieve?

The Greek words that are translated "anger" in these verses come from the root word *orge*. *Orge* is "anger as a state of mind; an emotion." Aristotle described this word as "desire with grief." *Orge* is sometimes appropriate, such as a justifiable abhorrence of evil or wrong. *Orge* is also associated with impulse. It may flare suddenly and be without intent. Let's look at a few more Scriptures so that we can better see the full counsel of God on the subject of anger.

Read Ephesians 4:31[88] and Colossians 3:8-10.[89] What do these Scriptures tell us to do with our anger?

Scripture tells us to place *orge* away from us; to lay it aside; and "if possible, so far as it depends on [us], [to] be at peace with all men" (Romans 12:18). Because we are human, our anger may flare on impulse, but we can keep anger from controlling us through God's Spirit.[T23]

There is another Greek word for anger—*thumos*. *Thumos* refers to the release of the emotional energy of strong anger. It is "passion, temper, outbursts, rage, wrath." *Thumos* is never appropriate for us; it is reserved for God's vengeance alone. In fact, *thumos* is used most often in the book of Revelation in reference to God's final judgment of the wicked.

Is the Christian to "be angry, yet not sin," to "be slow to anger," or to "put away anger" altogether? Let's examine one more Scripture before we answer.

## POINT OF INTEREST:[T23]

THE REMEDY FOR ANGER—When we're angry, we often feel that our anger would be satisfied if we could vindicate or defend ourselves. The antidote for anger, however, is not vindication but forgiveness. Being able to forgive is one of the highest forms of self-control for "it is [a man's] glory to overlook a transgression" (Proverbs 19:11).

In Proverbs 17:9 Solomon said, "He who covers a transgression seeks love." The ability to truly forgive is rooted in love for "love covers a multitude of sins" (1 Peter 4:8). Hatred, on the other hand, stirs up strife.

Scripture counsels us to have the kind of integrity that offers grace instead of revenge and to "overcome evil with good" (Romans 12:21). It is demonic to return evil for good, human to return evil for evil or good for good, but divine to return good for evil. This divine response (manifested in the life and death of Christ) is impossible for us to fulfill in the flesh. Only Christ can do it in us and through us as we walk in His Spirit and let Him take care of any wrong doing. He alone is the moral governor of the uni-verse, and He is the one who redresses wrongs.

*For further study:*
Proverbs 20:22, 24:19
Matthew 5:43-48
Romans 12:9-21
1 Peter 2:18-24
1 John 2:11-12

16-23,25-26 But I say, walk by the Spirit, and you will not carry out the desire of the flesh. For the flesh . . . and the Spirit . . . are in opposition to one another, so that you may not do the things that you please. But if you are led by the Spirit, you are not under the Law. Now the deeds of the flesh are evident, which are: immorality, impurity, sensuality, idolatry, sorcery, enmities, strife, jealousy, outbursts of anger, disputes, dissensions, factions, envying, drunkenness, carousing, and things like these, of which I forewarn you just as I have forewarned you that those who practice such things shall not inherit the kingdom of God. But the fruit of the Spirit is love, joy, peace, patience, kindness, goodness, faithfulness, gentleness, self-control; against such things there is no law. . . . If we live by the Spirit, let us also walk by the Spirit. Let us not become boastful, challenging one another, envying one another.

Read Galatians 5:16-23,25-26⁹⁰ and answer the following questions:

What two opponents are at war?

- 

- 

What will the deeds of the flesh keep us from inheriting?

What keeps us from carrying out desires of the flesh?

If we are led by the Spirit, what are we *not* under?

Why?

Life will always be full of frustrations, disappointments, and irritations; and the flesh will tend to react in ways that do not bring glory to God. The anger-related deeds of the flesh from Galatians 5:16-26 are listed below. Beside each "deed," write down one or two characteristics of the fruit of the Spirit that would render that deed inoperable. The first one is done for you.

| Deeds of the Flesh | Fruit of the Spirit |
| --- | --- |
| Enmities (hatred; hostility) | love |
| Strife (quarreling) | |
| Jealousy (zealous; argumentative) | |
| Outbursts of anger (*thumos*) | |
| Disputes (rivalry; selfish ambition) | |
| Dissensions (relational splits) | |
| Factions (taking sides; heresies) | |
| Envy (resentment; coveting) | |

We cannot both hate and love; both quarrel and be at peace. We cannot lash out in anger and be kind; burn

hot with jealous zeal and experience gentleness. Furthermore, we cannot walk in the Spirit and at the same time operate in ways that incite anger and envy in others.[T24] The flesh and the Spirit simply cannot coexist because the fruit of the Spirit lifts life to a plane that is not only higher than the deeds of the flesh, but far superior to the works of the Law.

Christians should get angry at whatever makes God angry—for the sake of His name, His kingdom, and His children! And Christians *will* get angry at times because of our human condition. But anger need not lead the Christian into sin, for we have been given the power over our flesh through the gift of His Spirit.

## BRINGING IT HOME . . .

1. When has someone demonstrated love for you by returning good for evil? In other words, when have you received forgiveness when you reacted with inappropriate anger to someone else?

2. How did you feel when this happened? What was the result?

3. Is there anyone you need to forgive? Let God enable you to do so right now. First deal with your feelings by being totally honest with the Lord. Once you are able to release your anger, go to the person and reconcile with him or her.

## CROSS REFERENCES:[T24]

ANGER—**Job 5:2:** For vexation slays the foolish man, and anger kills the simple.

**Job 36:13:** But the godless in heart lay up anger; they do not cry for help when He binds them.

**Psalm 37:8:** Cease from anger, and forsake wrath; do not fret, it leads only to evildoing.

**Proverbs 15:1:** A gentle answer turns away wrath, but a harsh word stirs up anger.

**Proverbs 29:8:** Scorners set a city aflame, but wise men turn away anger.

**Proverbs 30:33:** For the churning of milk produces butter, . . . so the churning of anger produces strife.

**Ecclesiastes 7:9:** Do not be eager in your heart to be angry, for anger resides in the bosom of fools.

**Romans 12:19:** Never take your own revenge, beloved, but leave room for the wrath of God, for it is written, "VENGEANCE IS MINE, I WILL REPAY," says the Lord.

**Ephesians 6:4:** And, fathers, do not provoke your children to anger; but bring them up in the discipline and instruction of the Lord.

### DAILY READING

Read Proverbs 16:1-33. Mark the verse that stands out most to you today.

# DAY 4

## THE WISE ARE PRUDENT

**[91] MATTHEW 7**

24-25 "Therefore everyone who hears these words of Mine, and acts upon them, may be compared to a wise man, who built his house upon the rock. And the rain descended, and the floods came, and the winds blew, and burst against that house; and yet it did not fall, for it had been founded upon the rock."

**[92] MATTHEW 25**

1-13 "Then the kingdom of heaven will be comparable to ten virgins. . . . And five of them were foolish, and five were prudent [phronimos]. For when the foolish took their lamps, they took no oil with them, but the prudent took oil in flasks along with their lamps. Now . . . at midnight there was a shout, 'Behold, the bridegroom! Come out to meet him.' Then all those virgins rose, and trimmed their lamps. And the foolish said to the prudent, 'Give us some of your oil, for our lamps are going out.' But the prudent answered, saying, 'No, there will not be enough for us and you too; go instead to the dealers and buy some for yourselves.' And while they were going away to make the purchase [of the oil], the bridegroom came, and those who were ready went in with him to the wedding feast; and the door was shut. And later the other virgins also came, saying, 'Lord, lord, open up for us.' But he answered and said, 'Truly I say to you, I do not know you.' Be on the alert then, for you do not know the day nor the hour [when Christ will return]."

Proverbs was written "To give prudence to the naive, to the youth knowledge and discretion" (Proverbs 1:4). Before studying what the Scriptures say about prudence, we need to understand the term. Two Hebrew words are translated "prudence." *Arum* means "to be sensible, shrewd, crafty, or cunning" and *bin* means "discerning or perceptive; having insight." The parallel Greek words for prudence are *phronimos*, meaning "practically wise, sensible, shrewd," and *sophron*, meaning "of sound mind; self-controlled, sensible."

If we looked up "shrewd," "crafty," or "cunning" in an English dictionary, we'd find that their primary meanings are negative. Webster defines these words as "mischievous, abusive, ominous, severe" and "actions marked by subtlety and guile; scheming or slyness." But "shrewedness" in Hebrew refers to "keen judgment, acute mental vision, and intellectual discernment." "Craftiness" refers to "being skillful and clever" and "cunning" means "dexterous skill and subtlety, as in inventing, devising, or executing." These Hebrew definitions reveal the true character of prudence with which "wisdom dwells" (Proverbs 8:12).

Read at least six (or more if you have time) of the proverbs below and write what you learn about the wise and the foolish in regard to prudence.

| | The Prudent | The Fool |
|---|---|---|
| 12:16 | | |
| 12:23 | | |
| 13:16 | | |
| 14:8 | | |
| 14:15 | | |
| 15:5 | | |
| 18:15 | | |
| 22:3 | | |

Proverbs characterizes prudent men and women as discrete and careful in their speech. Even though their wisdom is apparent by their behavior, they don't discuss improprieties or flaunt their knowledge. The prudent work at understanding themselves as well as understanding others. Before acting (or reacting), they evaluate information and discern truth. When justly reproved, they accept it. The prudent consider the potential consequences before acting. They seek knowledge and avoid evil.

In contrast, the foolish indiscriminately vent their anger and expose their ignorance. They're both deceptive and easily deceived, believing everything at face value. Fools align themselves with foolish and wicked companions. They reject reproof and pay a high price for their foolishness.

## DILIGENCE

A characteristic closely related to prudence is diligence. Diligence in the Hebrew is *charuts*, meaning "incisive, sharp, determined, eager." The parallel Greek word for diligence is *spoudazo*, meaning "eager, making every effort." In Proverbs, prudence and diligence are both characteristics of wisdom. In the New Testament, prudence and diligence are characteristics of Christ and, therefore, characteristics of His followers.[T25]

Jesus taught the importance of prudence and biblical shrewdness in parables (biblical principles taught in story form). Read the parables in Matthew 7:24-25[91] and excerpts of Matthew 25:1-13.[92]

Using the Greek and Hebrew definitions given previously, list some ways that the wise man in Matthew 7 showed prudence or diligence.

How did the five wise virgins in Matthew 25:1-13 show prudence or diligence?

**POINT OF INTEREST:**[T25]
THE REWARDS OF DILIGENCE AND PRUDENCE—When I (Ken) was at Oxford, I spent a year figuring out what my dissertation topic would be. I went to Oxford with a topic in mind but soon realized that the research would lead to some dead ends. (Nothing is worse than being roped with a dissertation and finding out in the middle of it that you're hitting a dead end.) So, I took advantage of the brain trust that was there; that is, I visited a lot of professors who didn't know me at all and who had no responsibilities to give me advice. Nevertheless, about a dozen of them agreed to let me just throw out some ideas about my topic and to tell me if they saw any problems with it I couldn't anticipate.

Plan A had to be modified. So did plans B through E. Plan F was a winner—but my overall work area had to be adjusted. Therefore, I had to change supervisors to find those suited to the change in topic. It was a lot of front-end work; but without that counsel, I would have run into major problems later on. Because these people were further along in their fields, they could predict the problems I would encounter.

It would have seemed easier to just begin writing. But prudence required that I find the right counsel and then heed it. The front-end leg work saved me hundreds of hours in research and writing time. Prudence paid big dividends!

**[93] ROMANS 12**

9-11 Let love be without hypocrisy. Abhor what is evil; cling to what is good. Be devoted to one another in brotherly love; give preference to one another in honor; not lagging behind in diligence, fervent in spirit, serving the Lord.

**[94] 2 PETER 1**

4-8,10-11 He has granted to us His precious and magnificent promises . . . [that] you might become partakers of the divine nature. . . . Now for this very reason also, applying all diligence, in your faith supply moral excellence . . . knowledge . . . self-control . . . perseverance . . . godliness . . . brotherly kindness . . . love. For if these qualities are yours and are increasing, they render you neither useless nor unfruitful in the true knowledge of our Lord Jesus Christ. . . . Therefore, brethren, be all the more diligent to make certain about His calling and choosing you; for as long as you practice these things, you will never stumble; for in this way the entrance into the eternal kingdom of our Lord and Savior Jesus Christ will be abundantly supplied to you.

**[95] HEBREWS 6**

10-12 God is not unjust so as to forget your work and the love which you have shown toward His name, in having ministered and in still ministering to the saints. . . . Show the same diligence so as to realize the full assurance of hope until the end, that you may not be sluggish, but imitators of those who through faith and patience inherit the promises.

The two parables from Matthew illustrate the principles of both prudence (keen discernment, intelligent perception, good judgment, insight) and diligence (skill, wise use of resources). Many passages in the New Testament call for Christians to exercise prudence and diligence in their walk with God.

Read Romans 12:9-11,[93] 2 Peter 1:4-8,10-11,[94] and Hebrews 6:10-12.[95] According to these Scriptures, to what areas are we to apply prudence and diligence?

Romans 12:9-11

2 Peter 1:4-8,10-11

Hebrews 6:10-12

What can the diligent expect to inherit, as mentioned in both 2 Peter and Hebrews?

When we exercise prudence and diligence in studying the Word and meditating on God, we are aiming our mental, spiritual, and material resources toward growing in the Christian faith. Prudence and diligence are the attributes by which the believer inherits the promises of God.

**BRINGING IT HOME . . .**

1. How are you doing in terms of being prudent and diligent? In the space below, list all the traits of the prudent and foolish you found on page 70. Then rate yourself on each trait using a scale of 1 to 5 (1 = never and 5 = always).

Prudent

Diligent

2. Spend time in prayer confessing your weaknesses or failures and thanking God for the growth He has brought about in your life. Ask God to help you become more like Him. What are some practical steps you can take related to the areas needing adjustment?

**DAILY READING**
Read Proverbs 17:1–18:8. Mark the verse that stands out most to you today.

## DAY 5

### THE WISE SEEK GODLY COUNSELORS

In unit 1 we looked at Proverbs 1:5[1] from the standpoint of hearing and embracing the Word. But the wise go beyond passive learning. Solomon knew and wrote about the importance of actively seeking guidance from those whose lives reflect wisdom and godliness: "A wise man will hear and increase in learning, and a man of understanding will acquire wise counsel." The wise are thoughtful in their decision-making and considerate of the impact their actions may have upon others.

The verses from Proverbs below contrast the results of obtaining godly counsel and not seeking guidance. List these results.

| | Guidance/Counsel | No Guidance |
|---|---|---|
| 11:14 | | |
| 13:10 | | |
| 15:22 | | |
| 19:20-21 | | |
| 24:6 | | |

Wisdom belongs to those who seek (and heed) wise counsel. God has provided us with four primary avenues from which we may gain understanding and insight—namely, Christian family members, the church body, the Bible, and the Spirit.[T26]

### CHRISTIAN FAMILY MEMBERS

As we saw in unit 1, God gave parents the mandate to teach their children the ways of God (Psalm 78:1-8[3]). This involves communicating the "what" and "why" of godly living as well as the "how."

In most cases, no one knows us better than our own family. They have seen us at our best and at our worst. Therefore, Christian parents and grandparents can help us apply the Word of God in specific ways to our lives.

---

[96]**TITUS 2**

2-8 Older men are to be temperate, dignified, sensible, sound in faith, in love, in perseverance. Older women likewise are to be reverent in their behavior, not malicious gossips, nor enslaved to much wine, teaching what is good, that they may encourage the young women to love their husbands, to love their children, to be sensible, pure, workers at home, kind, being subject to their own husbands, that the word of God may not be dishonored. Likewise urge the young men to be sensible; in all things show yourself to be an example of good deeds, with purity in doctrine, dignified, sound in speech which is beyond reproach, in order that the opponent may be put to shame, having nothing bad to say about us.

## THE CHURCH (THE BODY OF CHRIST)

In unit 1 we also looked at the limitations of human wisdom and the value of divine wisdom that is ours only through Christ. Through the gifts of the Spirit, God has equipped the body of Christ to build up, encourage, and nurture each other in the walk of faith. The church body, then, is an important resource for obtaining godly counsel.[T26]

Read Titus 2:2-8.[96] From whom are younger women and men supposed to learn?

What common characteristic does Paul tell each age group to exhibit or to be?

Christians gain wisdom and accrue "lessons learned" as they walk with God. More mature Christians are obligated by Scripture to share what they've learned with Christians who are newer in the faith. And regardless of their age or their years as a Christian, Paul tells everyone to be "sensible" (in Greek, *sophron*). As we said in our last study, *sophron* means "of sound mind; self-controlled; prudent." Sensible youth will listen to wise mentors who can help them avoid foolish mistakes. Sensible older Christians will continue to learn and grow. They also will counsel younger Christians in an attempt to help them avoid pain and heartache.

Scripture paints a detailed picture of the ideal mentor. This is important to know if you counsel others or are in need of godly wisdom. Consider the following texts:

> **1 Timothy 3:2-7:** An overseer, then, must be above reproach, the husband of one wife, temperate, prudent, respectable, hospitable, able to teach, not addicted to wine or pugnacious, but gentle, uncontentious, free from the love of money. He must be one who manages his own household well, keeping his children under control with all dignity . . . and not a new convert. . . . And he must have a good reputation with those outside the church.

### POINT OF INTEREST:[T26]

GETTING GODLY COUNSEL—Now and then we face potentially life-changing decisions that make us wish we could see into the future. We can't, of course, but wisdom tells us something we can do—get godly counsel in advance! The wise seek out others who have been through similar experiences and have learned something in the process.

Generally, most of us look for counselors who have been successful in a related area—education, career, marriage, children, or finances. But we must be careful. Successful people often think their achievements are based on their innate superiority to others. Generally, the most valuable counsel will come from those who have learned from their own experiences. They've made mistakes, reasoned through the causes, and gained valuable insight. They've applied what they've learned, made corrections, and experienced an outcome that has been tested by fire—something that sets it above the routine and the ordinary.

These are the counselors you need. And while they are scarce, they are well worth pursuing. Godly counsel is a gift from God that we should be careful to take advantage of in our lives.

*For further study:*
1 Kings 12:1-15

**97 HEBREWS 4**

12 For the word of God is living and active and sharper than any two-edged sword, and piercing as far as the division of soul and spirit, of both joints and marrow, and able to judge the thoughts and intentions of the heart.

**98 COLOSSIANS 3**

16 Let the word of Christ richly dwell within you, with all wisdom teaching and admonishing one another with psalms and hymns and spiritual songs, singing with thankfulness in your hearts to God.

**99 PSALM 119**

38 Establish Thy word to Thy servant, as that which produces reverence for Thee.

89 Forever, O LORD, Thy word is settled in heaven.

105 Thy word is a lamp to my feet, and a light to my path.

**100 REVELATION 19**

11,13 And I saw heaven opened; and behold, a white horse, and He who sat upon it is called Faithful and True. . . . and His name is called The Word of God.

**101 ISAIAH 11**

2 And the Spirit of the LORD will rest on Him, the spirit of wisdom and understanding, the spirit of counsel and strength, the spirit of knowledge and the fear of the LORD.

**102 ISAIAH 9**

6 For a child will be born to us, a son will be given to us; and the government will rest on His shoulders; and His name will be called Wonderful Counselor, Mighty God, Eternal Father, Prince of Peace.

Titus 1:7-9: For the overseer must be above reproach as God's steward, not self-willed, not quick-tempered . . . not fond of sordid gain, but . . . loving what is good, sensible, just, devout, self-controlled, holding fast the faithful word which is in accordance with the teaching, that he may be able both to exhort in sound doctrine and to refute those who contradict.

**THE BIBLE**

Another avenue for counsel is the Word of God. While you are studying Proverbs, you are receiving counsel from all the Scriptures you are reading—those in Proverbs as well as those from the rest of the Word.

The Word of God is powerful. Read Hebrews 4:12[97] and Colossians 3:16.[98] What can the Word of God do? How is the Word to be used?

The Word of God is a plumb line against which all else is measured; therefore, it can judge the thoughts and intentions of the heart. The indwelling Word produces wisdom by which we teach and admonish one another.

David knew the value of the Word of God. Read his appraisal of the counsel of the Word from Psalm 119[99] and summarize the *work* of the Word in our lives:

The Word of God is a sure Word, and it never changes. The Word is God's standard of holiness. It illumines us and produces reverence for Him. Read Revelation 19:11,13.[100] Why are the Scriptures so powerful and so perfect in counsel? Of whom does this passage speak?

In Proverbs 8:14, Wisdom says, "Counsel is mine and sound wisdom; I am understanding." Jesus, the Wisdom of God, is the Word made flesh. When we come to the Word, then, we need to realize that we are encountering the very mind of Christ. Read Proverbs 16:20.

## THE SPIRIT

The Word of God by the Spirit of God counsels specifically when our choices relate to godliness, sin issues, right relationships, ethics, or morals. The Word can also counsel specifically when our choices are directional such as vocational, marital, or financial. For example, Scripture may seem to jump out at us as we are reading and we somehow realize that the passage addresses our concerns. That inner prompting is the work of the Spirit interacting with God's Word to instruct us in the way we should go.

Read Proverbs 16:1-3,9. Who makes plans?


Who makes plans succeed?


Read Isaiah 11:2.[101] What attributes of the Spirit of the Lord contribute to successful planning?


Read Isaiah 9:6.[102] The Lord Himself will guide us through His Spirit if we yield to His will, for counsel and knowledge are His attributes. We are free to plan, but we are foolish if we don't submit those plans to God for correction or adjustment (or abandonment) as He sees fit (Jeremiah 10:23). If we are wise, then, we will seek His counsel from all the avenues available to us. He will establish His plans in our lives.

## BRINGING IT HOME . . .

1. When faced with a major decision, what is your first course of action? (Be totally honest.) Then what other steps do you usually take before reaching a conclusion? Once you've made a decision, what do you do if things do not work out as you thought they would?


2. What decisions are you currently facing? List them. For each one, name someone whose godly counsel would be helpful. Include those who are good models of success as well as those who have wrestled with a similar situation that they overcame. Seek God's input and then contact your potential counselors.

## DAILY READING

Read Proverbs 18:9–19:4. Mark the verse that stands out most to you today.

*To the leader: As the group is gathering have each person write a promise of God on the board.*

1. God is faithful to His promises and to His character whether we believe it or not. Our belief or lack of belief does not change God, but it has a profound impact on us. Sometimes the routine of living lulls us into not noticing where God is at work. Use the list of promises on the board and the following questions to prompt a time of sharing specific examples of God's faithfulness.
   - What are some daily demonstrations of God's faithfulness to the entire world (things such as the sun rising)?
   - What are some demonstrations of God's faithfulness to His body (the church)?
   - What are some evidences of God's faithfulness in your life right now?
   - How do you see the faithfulness of God in the lives of family members and friends?

2. Control of self under the power of the Holy Spirit is a key to living a victorious Christian life. This means saying no to ourselves, confessing our sin, and taking responsiblity for the consequences.
   - In areas of recurring temptation what practical steps have you taken to escape?
   - Discuss the following statement: Confession benefits us (rather than God) because it makes real in our experience what is already true in our position in Christ. Do you agree or disagree? Why?
   - In James 5:16 we are told to "confess your sins to one another, and pray for one another." What do you think this verse means? What is the value of mutual confession in the body of Christ? What is the difference between scriptural confession and airing our "dirty laundry"?

3. For each of the following scenarios determine if the person is demonstrating anger *(orgre)* or rage *(thumos)*. Is the expression of anger appropriate or inappropriate? What steps can the person take toward handling his or her feelings in a biblical and/or productive way?

   - Colleen and Mike have been married for five years. Even on their honeymoon they began having conflict. Mike would agree to do something (like make dinner reservations) but wouldn't carry through (so they'd have a two-hour wait). Now it's not uncommon for Mike to agree to get their three-year-old son from daycare at a specific time and arrive an hour late or not at all. At first Colleen was very patient, simply expressing her disappointment and suggesting that Mike do better in the future. Now she finds herself feeling angry with Mike most of the time and she often berates him for his poor performance.

   - Joe is an energetic, single professional. He serves on the deacon board at his church, volunteers with several community projects, and strives for excellence at the office, often working sixty-hour weeks. He has no time to waste or to wait. He's easily angered when others are late or when they get in his way. Earlier tonight another driver pulled in front of him and Joe hit the gas, swerved around the offender, and shouted, "You idiot!" When Cal arrived at the meeting ten minutes late, Joe gave him a nasty look and pointed to his watch. When leaving, Joe leaned over and whispered to Cal, "If I were God, I'd fire you."

4. To see a good description of prudent and diligent actions, read Luke 14:28-31. How can the principles of counting the cost and seeking wise counsel be applied in each of these situations?
   - Buying and financing a home
   - Investing a portion of your income each month
   - Planning a vacation
   - Determining how to care for an aging parent
   - Starting a business
   - Caring for a child with special needs such as A.D.D. or a physical or mental disability

Close with a time of praise for all the ways God shows His faithfulness day in and day out.

# INTRODUCTION TO UNIT 4
## COMMUNICATION AND CHARACTER

*Destination: To better appreciate the power of words and to understand the biblical approach to developing good communication skills.*

Aren't regional differences delightful! When I (Gail) am traveling south, I like to stop in Cordell, Georgia. The southern drawl of the locals is so strong there, it makes this Tennesseean feel like a northerner. Some of the older gentlemen still tip their hats to the ladies and most everyone is helpful and friendly. The town just seems to communicate welcome.

We communicate to others in many ways, but none is more important than speech. The things that come out of our mouths largely define who we are. The words we choose and the manner in which we say them tells something about our upbringing, our personality, and even our current mood. Words reveal our integrity (or lack thereof) as we become known as a person of truth or a liar, as one who keeps his or her word or breaks it. Moreover, our words have an incredible impact on others. Words can build people up or tear them down.

Some say we speak an average of between ten thousand and twenty thousand words daily. That's a little book. Because the average person doesn't read even one book a year, there's an obvious disproportion between input and output; and it shows sometimes in a lack of content in our discourses throughout the day.

We rarely stop to consider the importance and power of words. But the power of words was keenly understood by the writers of Proverbs. In fact, there are more than 150 proverbs that relate to the way we speak to one another. For this unit, we will examine a number of representative proverbs concerning speech. The first four days will focus on words of instruction, words that destroy, words that seduce, and words that edify. On day 5, we'll examine the limitations of our words.

As you work through this unit, make a conscious effort to pay attention to your own words throughout the day. Note your own patterns of speech.

- What is your tone?

- Do you tend to instruct or exhort?

- Do your speech habits build up or destroy?

Ask God to reveal how you use language and to show you how to be more effective for Him in communicating to others.

# DAY 1

## WORDS OF INSTRUCTION

**[103] JOHN 12**

47-49 [Jesus said] "And if anyone hears My sayings, and does not keep them, I do not judge him; for I did not come to judge the world, but to save the world. He who rejects Me, and does not receive My sayings, has one who judges him; the word I spoke is what will judge him at the last day. For I did not speak on My own initiative, but the Father Himself who sent Me has given Me commandment, what to say, and what to speak."

**[104] HEBREWS 12**

6-11 "FOR THOSE WHOM THE LORD LOVES HE DISCIPLINES, AND HE SCOURGES EVERY SON WHOM HE RECEIVES." It is for discipline that you endure; God deals with you as with sons; for what son is there whom his father does not discipline? But if you are without discipline . . . then you are illegitimate children and not sons. Furthermore, we had earthly fathers . . . [who] disciplined us for a short time as seemed best to them, but He disciplines us for our good, that we may share His holiness. All discipline for the moment seems not to be joyful, but sorrowful; yet to those who have been trained by it, afterwards it yields the peaceful fruit of righteousness.

**[105] 1 CORINTHIANS 11**

32 But when we are judged, we are disciplined by the Lord in order that we may not be condemned along with the world.

In Proverbs 22:17-21, Solomon admonishes his son (and us), "Incline your ear and hear the words of the wise, and apply your mind to my knowledge; for it will be pleasant if you keep them within you, that they may be ready on your lips. So that your trust may be in the LORD. . . . Have I not written to you excellent things of counsels and knowledge, to make you know the certainty of the words of truth?"

The purpose of Proverbs—indeed, the very essence of all Scripture—is spiritual and moral instruction. Without spiritual and moral instruction, we are (by default) given over to the ways of death. Our sin nature is a moral "marsh" that traps and confuses us. We are blind to our need of wisdom and will never pursue it unless we are taught to do so.

Read Proverbs 1:20-33. To whom does Wisdom call?

What will Wisdom pour out?

What will Wisdom make known?

Read Proverbs 8:6-17. What is Wisdom offering?

Now read John 12:47-49.[103] What is Jesus offering?

Our instruction in wisdom comes in the form of words—from God's spoken word to the Living Word—penned by men as they were moved by the Holy Spirit. We must receive these words as instruction from the very heart of the Father, for they are the standard against which we will be judged.

## RECEIVING INSTRUCTION

We may not pursue wisdom, but wisdom will pursue us through creation and through the medium of words—words from parents, grandparents, teachers, and mentors; words from authors, evangelists, and pastors; and, most importantly, words from Scripture. Our job is to receive Wisdom's words of instruction, reproof, rebuke, and encouragement. Read the following verses from Proverbs and write what you learn about our responsibility for receiving words of instruction.

**Instruction**

1:23

4:5

19:27

22:17

23:12

23:23

As we saw in unit 1, "receiving" is not a passive openness but an active, aggressive participation in the pursuit of the knowledge of God and of wisdom from above. These proverbs tell us to be attentive to truth, to remember truth, to buy truth, and to apply truth to our lives—even if truth hurts and comes in the form of reproof or discipline.[T27] Read Hebrews 12:6-11[104] and 1 Corinthians 11:32.[105]

Who does the Lord discipline?

How does He deal with them?

Give at least three reasons for God's discipline according to these verses:

- 
- 
- 

What does the discipline yield?

**106 LUKE 17**
3 "Be on your guard! If your brother sins, rebuke him; and if he repents, forgive him."

**107 MATTHEW 18**
15-17 "And if your brother sins, go and reprove him in private. . . . But if he does not listen to you, take one or two more with you. . . . And if he refuses to listen to them, tell it to the church; and if he refuses to listen even to the church, let him be to you as a Gentile and a tax-gatherer."

**108 EPHESIANS 4**
14-15 As a result, we are no longer to be children, . . . carried about by every wind of doctrine, . . . but speaking the truth in love, we are to grow up in all aspects into Him, who is the head, even Christ.

What is the goal of wisdom (see page 40)?

God may speak words of rebuke to our heart through the Holy Spirit's convicting power or He may make His Word alive to us. God may allow circumstances to discipline us or may send a brother or sister in the body of Christ to speak words of truth, instruction, or reproof to us. He may also send us to speak words of truth and reproof to other believers.

## SPEAKING WORDS OF TRUTH AND REPROOF

Most of us are better at giving instruction (at least to people in our comfort zones) than we are at receiving instruction. But exhorting (or admonishing others) is not always easy, especially when repercussions are likely. Nevertheless, Scripture gives us certain mandates to speak words of instruction or reproof when circumstances call for it.[T28] Read some of those circumstances from the following proverbs and write what you learn in the space below.

### Giving Instruction or Reproof

12:17

24:25

31:8

31:9

God's people are not to keep silent about injustice, oppression, abuse, or sin. Read the following proverbs. Write the reactions one can expect from those reproved.

### Reactions to Reproof

9:8

19:25

28:23

Those who have spiritual maturity, knowledge, and wisdom are commanded to speak out, reproving others and instructing them in righteousness and truth.

Read Luke 17:3,[106] Matthew 18:15-17,[107] and Ephesians 4:14-15.[108] Then review 2 Timothy 3:16.[62]

What must be the basis for evaluating a need for reproof?

What heart attitude do we need to have when we reprove?

We are instructed by the Word to instruct others *in* the Word and *through* the Word. But we are never to speak out on the basis of our own personal standards. The caution is this: Speak only the truth of God and speak only in love. Then leave the outcome to God.

## BRINGING IT HOME . . .

1. In Proverbs 27:6 Solomon wrote, "Faithful are the wounds of a friend." Do you have a friend who knows you and loves you enough to speak truth, even when it hurts?

   If so, thank God for that person (or those people). Take a few minutes to pray for your friend(s) in the areas of mutual accountability. Either drop a note or make a phone call to each one to express your thankfulness for your friendship.

   If not, ask God to bring another Christian into your life to help hold you accountable to God's instruction. This type of relationship takes time to develop and to nurture. It may be the person is already in your life and you just need to initiate the idea of accountability.

2. What recent words of instruction do you need to act on? How can you apply these words today?

## POINT OF INTEREST:[T28]

THE CONTENTIOUS PERSON— One of the best pieces of management advice I (Gail) ever received was from my division director who said, "If you ever find that your staff is staying in a continual state of agitation, ferret out the instigator immediately. As quickly as possible, isolate, transfer, or terminate that employee."

Perhaps my director had learned this lesson the hard way. Or perhaps he had read Proverbs. Either way, I found his advice to be right on target. And to my surprise, the instigators have never been difficult to spot. Contentious people stand out in any crowd!

## DAILY READING

Read Proverbs 19:5–20:9. Mark the verse that stands out most to you today.

# DAY 2

## WORDS THAT DESTROY

In Proverbs 18:21, Solomon wrote, "Death and life are in the power of the tongue, and those who love it will eat its fruit." When we really consider the force of the things we say, we are awed at the tremendous power of words for evil and for good. Read the proverbs below and record what you learn of the power of words for evil.

### Evil Words

10:11

11:9

16:27

16:28

25:18

Note the destructive and consuming qualities surrounding the objects that are compared to harsh and evil words (clubs, sharp arrow, thrust of a sword, scorching fire). Cruel words can do more damage than weapons of war and violent aggression. In fact, we get the word "sarcasm" from the Greek word *sarkinos,* which means "cutting the flesh."

Read James 3:7-8,10.[109] What can't be tamed or trained not to speak words of destruction?

How does James describe the tongue?

Based on Galatians 5:15-16[110] and James 5:9,[111] what are the imminent dangers when we "bite and devour" and complain against one another?

▪

▪

Who is watching "at the door" when we complain against our brother?

How can we keep from criticizing our brother unfairly?

---

[109] **JAMES 3**

7-8,10 For every species of beasts and birds, of reptiles and creatures of the sea, is tamed, and has been tamed by the human race. But no one can tame the tongue; it is a restless evil and full of deadly poison. . . . From the same mouth come both blessing and cursing. My brethren, these things ought not to be this way.

[110] **GALATIANS 5**

15-16 But if you bite and devour one another, take care lest you be consumed by one another.

But I say, walk by the Spirit, and you will not carry out the desire of the flesh.

[111] **JAMES 5**

9 Do not complain, brethren, against one another, that you yourselves may not be judged; behold, the Judge is standing right at the door.

[112] **GALATIANS 5**

25-26 If we live by the Spirit, let us also walk by the Spirit. Let us not become boastful, challenging one another, envying one another.

[113] **JAMES 3**

14-16 But if you have bitter jealousy and selfish ambition in your heart, do not be arrogant and so lie against the truth. This wisdom is not that which comes down from above, but is earthly, natural, demonic. For where jealousy and selfish ambition exist, there is disorder and every evil thing.

## GOSSIP AND SLANDER

Gossip may be simply discussing things that are really none of our concern or revealing relatively benign confidences that a trustworthy person would keep.[T29] Left unchecked, however, gossip can quickly evolve into some level of slander. Slander can be either an outright lie or a damaging truth that should not have been repeated. In either case, one or more persons are injured.

Read the following verses from Proverbs, noting insights about slander and gossip.

### Gossip and Slander

10:18

12:19

20:19

30:10

Gossip is described in Proverbs as "morsels [that] go down into the innermost parts of the body." When you hear negative information about someone, you tend not to forget it; it leaves a residue on the way you see the slandered person from that point on—even if you later learn that the gossip was untrue.

Read Matthew 18:15-17.[107] There is a major difference between lovingly confronting a brother or sister in Christ with the truth and spreading damaging information (whether true or false) about that person to others. What difference do you see?

Scripture tells us not to associate with a gossip. The wisdom in that is obvious—it's the only way to protect your own confidences from being divulged. Don't be deceived! Eventually, you will become the source of the gossiper's "morsels."

Read Galatians 5:25-26[112] and James 3:14-16.[113] What do you see in these verses that often motivates gossipers and slanderers?

### HISTORY & CULTURE:[T29]
THE RIGHT TO OUR REPUTATION—

There are four fundamental rights in the decalog of the mosaic law (that is, the Ten Commandments). These are:

- The right to your life. ("You shall not murder"—Exodus 20:13.)
- The right to fidelity in marriage. ("You shall not commit adultery"—20:14.)
- The right to your property. ("You shall not steal"—20:15.)
- The right to your reputation. ("You shall not bear false witness"—20:16.)

Few people would consider slander heinous enough to be included with murder, adultery, and stealing. That may be because we rarely stop to consider the long-range consequences of ruining another person's good name. Obviously, we should consider the sin of slander more seriously. God does.

[114] **1 TIMOTHY 4**

1-2 But the Spirit explicitly says that in later times some will fall away from the faith, paying attention to deceitful spirits and doctrines of demons, by means of the hypocrisy of liars seared in their own conscience as with a branding iron.

6-7 In pointing out these things to the brethren, you will be a good servant of Christ Jesus, constantly nourished on the words of the faith and of the sound doctrine which you have been following. But have nothing to do with worldly fables fit only for old women. On the other hand, discipline yourself for the purpose of godliness.

Because they grow out of jealousy and envy, gossip and slander bring us a certain perverse pleasure—as if our value were increased by the process of devaluing another person. In reality, however, the slanderer is discounted right along with the one whom she or he slanders. It's like vandalism—a crime where nobody wins.

## WORDS OF CONTENTION AND STRIFE

Contention is the verbal bemoanings of the discontent—complaining, harping, nagging, whining.

Read Proverbs 19:13. To what is the contentious wife compared?



According to Proverbs 26:21 what are contentious men like?



Strife, by the way, is the fighting and quarreling that results from contention, gossip, slander, or harsh speech.[T30] It is the retaliation that results from wounding others and creating an atmosphere where they need to defend or protect themselves. Read the following verses from Proverbs and record what you learn about contention and strife.

### Contention and Strife

15:18

16:27

17:14

20:3

22:10

In summary, what differences do you see between disagreement and strife, according to these verses from Proverbs?



There is a place for genuine disagreement. But strife and quarreling usually involve anger and loss of emotional control. They create more "heat" than "light." In the above proverbs several character types who initiate

contention and strife are mentioned, namely, the fool, the contentious person, the scoffer, the hot-tempered person, and the worthless person. The "fools" in Proverbs 20:3 are the *evilim*—the same fools from our key verse (Proverbs 1:7⁴) who despise wisdom and instruction, oppose spiritual matters, and love folly.

### LYING AND DECEIVING WORDS

Lying, deceiving, and being a false witness indicate pre-meditated, intentional fabrication. Read the following verses from Proverbs. What do they teach us about liars and false witnesses?

**Liars and Deceivers**

12:22

17:4

19:5

Within a few years after Jesus died, John wrote that those who did not acknowledge Jesus as coming in the flesh were deceivers and the antichrist, and that many of them had already gone out into the world (2 John 1:7). Read 1 Timothy 4:1-2,6-7.[114] Do you see similarities between the "later times" Paul described and our world today? What should you do, according to this passage?

### BRINGING IT HOME . . .

1. None of us likes to admit we personally deal with evil words, gossip, slander, contention, strife, or lying. But God knows and cares. Ask Him to reveal any words you have spoken that have caused strife or pain. If you haven't already done so, go to those who were affected (you should confess even if they don't know) and ask forgiveness. If needed, also go to those with whom you shared and retract your words.

2. Also, ask God to give you a sensitive and honest perception of your speech. Are you more likely to speak edifying or destructive words? Do you encourage or discourage? Seek God's help in reversing any negative patterns.

### POINT OF INTEREST:[T30]

WORDS CAN TOO HURT ME!— When I (Ken) was eight years old, some kids ganged up on me and called me names. I can see myself, even now, standing there on the sidewalk in Dumont, New Jersey, saying, "Sticks and stones may break my bones, but words can never hurt me." Even as I said it, however, I knew that phrase was lame. Those words did hurt—they cut to the bone and made such a mark that they remain a vivid and stinging memory, even after forty years!

Unkind words have tremendous power to sting. We are most vulnerable to speaking unkindly when we're emotionally stretched or out of control. We strike out at others—usually those we love—in an attempt to relieve our own frustrations, then we immediately see the painful impact of our injurous words. We've punished the innocent! We may greatly regret what we've said, but it's too late. Even an apology (though due) cannot undo all the damage. Remember, "A closed mouth gathers no foot." We must be cautious about our words.

### DAILY READING

Read Proverbs 20:10–21:31. Mark the verse that stands out most to you today.

# DAY 3

## WORDS THAT SEDUCE

We think that harsh words, slander, and gossip, and words of contention, strife, deception, and lying are all extremely destructive—and they are. But perhaps even more deadly are words of seduction. Seductive words give the appearance of building us up, but they are really bait to lure us into compromise. As Solomon said in Proverbs 29:5, "A man who flatters his neighbor is spreading a net for his steps." Often it isn't until the trap has sprung that we realize what a terrible mistake we've made. By then, there may be irreparable damage.

### WORDS OF BOASTING AND FLATTERY

We all dislike being around people who are always tooting their own horns or finding significance in the important names they drop. The basis of such boasting is pride, and pride is sin. In fact, James 4:16 says, "You boast in your arrogance; all such boasting is evil." Instead of achieving self-promotion, however, boasting is self-destructive; for God's Word promises, "Everyone who exalts himself shall be humbled" (Luke 14:11).

Before both God and others, the boaster damages himself. The flatterer, on the other hand, damages other people as well. Read the following verses from Proverbs and note why flatterers make dangerous companions.

### Flatterers

7:21

26:28

28:23

29:5

Read Romans 16:17-18.[115] What does smooth and flattering speech do?

Read Jude 1:16.[116] What is the intent of flattery according to Jude?

How are we to respond to flatterers according to Romans 16?

**ROAD MAP** sidebar:

[115] **ROMANS 16**

17-18 Now I urge you, brethren, keep your eye on those who cause dissensions and hindrances contrary to the teaching which you learned, and turn away from them. For such men are slaves, not of our Lord Christ but of their own appetites; and by their smooth and flattering speech they deceive the hearts of the unsuspecting.

[116] **JUDE 1**

16 These are grumblers, finding fault, following after their own lusts; they speak arrogantly, flattering people for the sake of gaining an advantage.

[117] **ACTS 13**

8-10 But Elymas the magician . . . was opposing them, seeking to turn the proconsul away from the faith. But Saul, who was also known as Paul . . . said, "You who are full of all deceit and fraud, you son of the devil, you enemy of all righteousness, will you not cease to make crooked [perverse] the straight ways of the Lord?"

What do you think is the difference between an encourager and a flatterer?[T31]

Flatterers are deceptive, full of guile, and manipulative. Flatterers *always* have an agenda. Telling another person what they want to hear when it isn't really true is a verbal bribe, even if the payoff is nothing more than personal popularity. We're often drawn to flatterers because we love the praise of others. But unless we want to find ourselves being used or taken advantage of in some way, we need to recognize *and turn away from* the flatterer.

## PERVERSE SPEECH

In both Hebrew and Greek, the words for "perverse" come from an idea of "being bent, distorted, twisted, or crooked." It means "to subvert; to turn upside down." Perverse speech, then, is verbalizing opposition to what's right, reasonable, or acceptable in order to turn others away from what's true or morally right. For an excellent portrait of a person of perverse speech, read Acts 13:8-10.[117] With Elymas in mind, read the following proverbs. Write what you learn about those whose speech (or tongue) is perverted.

### Perverse Speech

8:13

10:31

16:28

16:30

19:1

Proverbs uses some pretty strong language regarding the perverted mouth; namely, God hates it! If we fear the Lord, we must hate perverse speech too. Look again at Acts 13:8-10.[117] In your own words write Paul's "in-his-face" description of Elymas, noting what Elymas was doing to the ways of the Lord.

**POINT OF INTEREST:**[T31]
ENCOURAGER OR FLATTERER—One of the gifts God gives His church is people who encourage us. An encourager has the ability (through the work of the Spirit) to help us press on in our Christian work and grow in our own use of spiritual gifts and ministries.

Even outside the body of Christ, there are people who seem oriented toward encouraging others. There's a key difference, however, between sincere encouragers and flatterers. Flatterers will have a self-serving agenda. Their interest in you is really an interest in themselves; their feigned attention is simply bait to achieve whatever end they have in mind. People who are good at flattery can lay a real trap for people who are needy or who are not very discerning.

Three things will help you avoid entrapment:

- Do not respond too quickly to those who offer generous praise. If you don't react immediately, flatterers will usually escalate their attention (because they have an end in view) and their flattery will eventually become obvious by its absurdity.
- Listen for reproof as well as praise. Because none of us is perfect, true exhorters will correct as well as encourage, offering gentle suggestions for improvement.
- Examine your own agenda. Perhaps you seek people who praise you because of pride or because of chronic low self-esteem. Ask God to help you find your significance in Him so that you are not vulnerable to flattering speech.

**[118] ACTS 20**

29-31 I know that after my departure savage wolves will come in among you, not sparing the flock; and from among your own selves men will arise, speaking perverse things, to draw away the disciples after them. Therefore be on the alert.

**[119] PHILIPPIANS 2**

14-16 Do all things without grumbling or disputing; that you may prove yourselves to be blameless and innocent, children of God above reproach in the midst of a crooked and perverse generation, among whom you appear as lights in the world, holding fast the word of life.

**[120] ROMANS 13**

13-14 Let us behave properly as in the day, not in carousing and drunkenness, not in sexual promiscuity and sensuality, not in strife and jealousy. But put on the Lord Jesus Christ, and make no provision for the flesh in regard to its lusts.

**[121] JAMES 1**

14-16 But each one is tempted when he is carried away and enticed by his own lust. Then when lust has conceived, it gives birth to sin; and when sin is accomplished, it brings forth death. Do not be deceived, my beloved brethren

**[122] 1 CORINTHIANS 10**

13 No temptation has overtaken you but such as is common to man; and God is faithful, who will not allow you to be tempted beyond what you are able, but with the temptation will provide the way of escape also, that you may be able to endure it.

The religious arena is a common source of perverse speech. People who are ignorant of biblical principles are easy prey for those who would draw them into belief systems that twist God's Word and set the unsuspecting on a course for hell. Although perverse speech is morally and spiritually corrupt in our culture, it is politically correct and it prevails. American colleges and universities are overrun with perverse speakers who discredit God's laws on the basis of their intellectual presumption. They oppose spiritual matters and hold divine wisdom in disdain. *They are fools!* Nevertheless, their perverse speech is seductive because it has academic sanctions and it follows prevailing human-centered ideologies.

Read Acts 20:29-31[118] and Philippians 2:14-16.[119] What are two things we can do to avoid being seduced by perverse speech?

- 
- 

If we know the Word of God, it will be a reference point against which we can gauge the uprightness of everything else that comes into our information base. We must be on the alert, however, holding fast to the Word of life and examining everything by God's standard.

## WORDS OF SENSUALITY

Our final category of seductive words concerns sensuality and sexual allure. Much of the first nine chapters of Proverbs is devoted to teaching the son wisdom in regard to sexual temptation and immorality.

Read Proverbs 5:3, 6:24, and 22:14 from appendix A. What tools do the adulteresses use to entice?

Now read Proverbs 7:6-10,21-27. What powerful images! Proverbs contrasts the *allure* of lust ("lips that drip honey; speech that is smoother than oil") with the *cost* of lust ("an ox to the slaughter; arrow pierces through his liver, ways descend to the chambers of death"). Here the young man is hardly a victim, however. In verse 8 we are told he deliberately took the way to the house of the adulteress—in the middle of the night. Sin was in his heart long before it was acted out in his flesh.

Read Romans 13:13-14,[120] James 1:14-16,[121] and Proverbs 2:1-17. Write below God's provisions for us to overcome temptations from seductive words.

Scripture tells us that if we are to be free from sexual sin, we must take every improper "thought captive to the obedience of Christ" (2 Corinthians 10:5). That is, we must not dwell on lustful thoughts or make provision for the flesh (as the young man did). Finally, we must feed on the Word of God, making our ear attentive to wisdom from above. Then, we will "walk in the way of good men [and women], and keep to the paths of the righteous" (Proverbs 2:20).

## BRINGING IT HOME . . .

1. Would others consider you a boaster or flatterer? Use the following questions to evaluate yourself:

   - Do I like to drop names of important or famous people I know?

   - Do I make sure others are aware of my contribution and achievements?

   - When I compliment others or point out their strengths, what do I expect in return?

2. What are some sources of perverse or seductive words in your life? Read 1 Corinthians 10:13.[122] What is the way of escape from these words that boast, flatter, pervert, or seduce? What practical steps do you need to take to eliminate words of perversion or seduction?

**DAILY READING**
Read Proverbs 22:1–23:11. Mark the verse that stands out most to you today.

# DAY 4

## WORDS THAT EDIFY

**123 MATTHEW 12**

36-37 "And I [ Jesus] say to you, that every careless word that men shall speak, they shall render account for it in the day of judgment. For by your words you shall be justified, and by your words you shall be condemned."

**124 MARK 7**

21-23 "For from within, out of the heart of men, proceed the evil thoughts, fornications, thefts, murders, adulteries, deeds of coveting and wickedness, as well as deceit, sensuality, envy, slander, pride and foolishness. All these evil things proceed from within and defile the man."

**125 1 SAMUEL 14**

27 Jonathan . . . put out the end of the staff that was in his hand and dipped it in the honeycomb, and put his hand to his mouth, and his eyes brightened.

**126 COLOSSIANS 4**

6 Let your speech always be with grace, seasoned, as it were, with salt, so that you may know how you should respond to each person.

In this unit so far, we've learned the destructive power of harsh words, slander, gossip, boasting, flattery, perverse speech, and sensual words. This covers a lot of territory. Destroying another person with our words is not just a problem in earthly relationships, it's a problem with eternal consequences.

Read Matthew 12:36-37.[123] For what shall we give an account in the day of judgment?

By what shall we be justified or condemned in the day of judgment?

According to Mark 7:21-23,[124] what do our words (and deeds) tell us about ourselves?

Read Proverbs 10:19-20 and 17:27-28 from appendix A. What's one way we can avoid being verbally destructive?

It's a fact of human depravity that we can't talk much without sinning. Speaking many words makes us stumble. Things in our imperfect hearts just come out—pride, arrogance, lack of love, hatred. It's a bit unnerving, then, to know that we will be judged by *every word* that comes out of our mouths! Most of us will regret far more of what we've said than what we've left unsaid. It is "wise unto eternity," therefore, for us to pause and reflect, exercise a little caution, and give ourselves a few seconds to think before we speak, especially when we're angry, frustrated, or tired. We must learn to weigh our words so that our speech will bring correction, healing, and growth rather than pain and destruction.[T32]

## WORDS OF GRACE AND KINDNESS

Read Proverbs 12:25, 15:4, 16:24, and 27:9. Words can, in themselves, have healing and life-giving power. A good word can build up, teach, and exhort. Kind words are like food for the human spirit—there's a sweetness to them. Proverbs 16:24 compares that sweetness to eating honey. Read 1 Samuel 14:27.[125] What happened to Jonathan's eyes when he ate the honey?

Jonathan was overcome with hunger and the weariness of war, but he was sufficiently revived by the honey to stay in the battle. The sweetness gave Jonathan renewed strength and energy. Words of encouragement can be a powerful restorer for the war-weary Christian, family member, or friend. We should be generous with words of sincere kindness and grace.

## WORDS OF PERSUASION AND PEACE

It's important to use words with the gentle and peaceable qualities described in Proverbs. This is especially true in times of confrontation and correction.

Read Proverbs 12:20, 16:21, and 25:15. What is the peace speaker's reward?

What increases persuasiveness?

What can a soft response do?

Read Colossians 4:6.[126] What should characterize our speech?

To what preservative is grace compared?

What will the practice of grace in our speech teach us?

**POINT OF INTEREST:[T32]**
ACCOUNTABILITY FOR OUR WORDS—When we stand before Him face to face, God will not be impressed with excuses but will deal with the reality of what is in our thoughts or what is the attitude of our hearts. There will be a day of accountability. It is important, therefore, to be guarded about what we say—to make sure that we will be able to fulfill whatever we promise. It's important to think before we speak and to let our words be few.

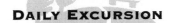
<sup>127</sup>**EPHESIANS 4**

29 Let no unwholesome word proceed from your mouth, but only such a word as is good for edification according to the need of the moment, that it may give grace to those who hear.

<sup>128</sup>**PSALM 15**

1-5 O LORD, who may abide in Thy tent? Who may dwell on Thy holy hill? He who walks with integrity, and works righteousness, and speaks truth in his heart. He does not slander with his tongue, nor does evil to his neighbor, nor takes up a reproach against his friend; in whose eyes a reprobate is despised, but who honors those who fear the LORD; he swears to his own hurt, and does not change; he does not put out his money at interest, nor does he take a bribe against the innocent. He who does these things will never be shaken.

Practicing gracious speech increases our effectiveness at encouragement, especially as we observe the results.<sup>T33</sup> Gracious speech can preserve a person and can perserve a relationship. Calm, rational, gracious words have more strength than words that are spoken in loud, harsh, and threatening tones. Soft answers have enough power to break the strongest resistance in another person. Moreover, calm speech, especially under duress, expresses a Christlikeness in us.

**TIMING OF WORDS**

Read Proverb 15:23. What is an important component of speech that really exhorts?

According to Ephesians 4:29,<sup>127</sup> what are the only kinds of words that we should speak?

What determines the content of the edifying words?

What should our words give to those who hear?

An important part of encouragement is that it must be appropriate to the occasion. As we are told in Proverbs 25:11, "Like apples of gold in settings of silver is a word spoken in right circumstances." Speaking a timely word requires us to listen intently to what people are saying, read their emotional state, and have an understanding of what they need in their particular circumstance. For example, it is an insensitive and hurtful thing to say to a grieving person, "It's time to get over it," or to a troubled person, "Just look on the bright side." Such words do not encourage but often create further despair. Even if we're not gifted at speech, we can learn to encourage others in the right manner and at the right time.

## WORDS OF RIGHTEOUSNESS AND TRUTH

Wisdom says of herself in Proverbs 8:8, "All the utterances of my mouth are in righteousness; there is nothing crooked or perverted in them." Read the following proverbs and write what you learn about those who speak in righteousness and listen to truth.

### Righteous and Truthful Speech

10:21

10:31

15:28

16:13

21:28

The common theme among these verses is that the speech of the righteous is both a source of spiritual nourishment and an example of caution and care. Remember, the goal of wisdom is a life of righteousness—in speech as well as in deed.

## BRINGING IT HOME . . .

1. List the names of family and friends who are in need of some special encouragement. Beside each name write down words of peace and grace you will share with them.

2. Read Psalm 15:1-5.[128] Record the characteristics of the one who abides in Christ. Pray through the list asking God to bring changes in your thoughts and heart so that your speech and conduct will conform to this picture of a righteous person.

## POINT OF INTEREST:[T33]

WORDS OF GRACE—There is an old joke about a man who told his wife on their wedding day that he loved her and that if he ever changed his mind, he'd let her know. We laugh because the joke exposes a common behavior. Wives often express their love verbally. Husbands don't, even though they, too, experience insecurity if their wives cease to verbalize their love.

We should treat all relationships as if each time together could be the last. If someone pops into our minds, we should immediately pray for them. Then we should call them up and tell them they were just in our thoughts and prayers—especially if our friends or loved ones have been experiencing discouragement or setbacks in their lives.

Words can be a powerful, rejuvenating tonic! If you love your spouse, child, parent, or friend, tell him or her. How often people regret not doing so—particularly after the person is gone. If you appreciate someone for doing something for you—teaching you something, impacting your life for good, or just living an exemplary life—tell them and tell them now.

## DAILY READING

Read Proverbs 23:12–24:20. Mark the verse that stands out most to you today.

# DAY 5

## WORDS HAVE LIMITATIONS

Our focus up to this point has been on the power of human speech, both for good and for harm. We've seen that good words rightly spoken are incredibly productive in the lives of others. When the need is encouragement, love, support, instruction, affirmation, or even loving admonishment and reproof, words can be deeds of kindness. We also learned that words carry tremendous power to inflict pain. Damaging words are an occasion of sin in themselves.

Words alone, however, are not all-encompassing; they have limitations. Words are useless unless they have substance, unless there's a responsive hearer, unless they are backed up by actions, and unless they are rooted in reality.[T34,T35] Even words of wisdom, by themselves, have limitations, many of which are imposed by the hearer.

Read Proverbs 1:20-33 from appendix A. What is Wisdom asking the simple, the scoffers, and the fools to do?

How do the simple, the scoffers, and the fools respond to Wisdom's call?

Wisdom is not forced on the foolish nor do her words fall simply on deaf ears. Instead, Wisdom is treated with open contempt and rejected. The simple, the scoffers, and the fools do not choose the fear of the Lord. They hate words of knowledge. They despise words of counsel and reproof—and they also reap the consequences. Read Proverbs 1:26-33 and briefly summarize.

### LIMITATIONS IN INSIGHT

Read 1 Corinthians 4:20.[129] The kingdom of God isn't just words, but also what?

---

**129 1 CORINTHIANS 4**

20 For the kingdom of God does not consist in words, but in power.

**130 1 CORINTHIANS 2**

12-13 Now we have received, not the spirit of the world, but the Spirit who is from God, that we might know the things freely given to us by God, which things we also speak, not in words taught by human wisdom, but in those taught by the Spirit, combining spiritual thoughts with spiritual words.

**131 1 CORINTHIANS 2**

11,14 For who among men knows the thoughts of a man except the spirit of the man, which is in him? Even so the thoughts of God no one knows except the Spirit of God. But a natural man does not accept the things of the Spirit of God; for they are foolishness to him, and he cannot understand them, because they are spiritually appraised.

**132 1 CORINTHIANS 2**

1-5 And when I came to you, brethren, I did not come with superiority of speech or of wisdom, proclaiming to you the testimony of God. For I determined to know nothing among you except Jesus Christ, and Him crucified. And I was with you in weakness and in fear and in much trembling. And my message and my preaching were not in persuasive words of wisdom, but in demonstration of the Spirit and of power, that your faith should not rest on the wisdom of men, but on the power of God.

Read 1 Corinthians 2:12-13.[130] What enables us to know the things given to us by God?

What does the Spirit combine?

Wisdom is described and illustrated in the Bible, but the words alone cannot make you wise. Not only must the words be heard (or read), they must be received with faith. Faith releases God's Spirit to give us insight into His Word and to help us walk in the Spirit.

## LIMITATIONS IN SHARING THE GOSPEL

Most of us Christians have made the mistake (at least once) of trying to *talk* someone else into accepting Christ—a person who was hurting, perhaps, or a loved one. We knew we had the answer to their deepest need, yet we were unable to convey it in words that would cause that person to be receptive to the gospel. It's like living out the old cliché of leading a thirsty horse to water and not being able to make him drink. What an exasperating experience!

There are limitations to our words when trying to share the gospel, and there are also limitations to the hearer's ability to respond.

Read 1 Corinthians 2:11,14.[131] What hinders the hearer from understanding the things of God?

Read 1 Corinthians 2:1-5.[132] What did Paul's message and preaching demonstrate?

What is the potential danger of eloquent speech or human wisdom?

On what basis must our faith rest?

---

**POINT OF INTEREST:**[T34]
WORDS WITHOUT ACTION—Words take on reality and relevance only when they are coupled with appropriate deeds. Talking about writing a book won't write it; talking about forgiving somebody won't make them forgiven; talking about meeting someone's need won't meet it. As Solomon says in Proverbs 14:23, "In all labor there is profit, but mere talk leads only to poverty."

Mere talk leads only to poverty in all kinds of circumstances. The most common string of words used without action (or with contradictory action) is "I love you." It may feel good to the speaker and may, for the moment, feel good to the hearer. But unless there are loving actions to back up the words, they are far better left unsaid.

**POINT OF INTEREST:**[T35]
IDLE THREATS AND EMPTY PROMISES—Words must elicit action or they are impotent. Within themselves, words cannot inflict punishment nor compel a response. Words spoken by those who have no authority or by those who have failed to carry out their threats or promises in the past are but sound and wind.

Parents who do not back up their words with action establish a precedence that young children quickly pick up on. It doesn't take long for the parents' words to become idle noises that astute children quickly learn to ignore.

**[133] JOHN 15**

7 "If you abide in Me, and My words abide in you, ask whatever you wish, and it shall be done for you."

**[134] PSALM 37**

3-7 Trust in the LORD, and do good; dwell in the land and cultivate faithfulness. Delight yourself in the LORD; and He will give you the desires of your heart. Commit your way to the LORD, trust also in Him, and He will do it. And He will bring forth your righteousness as the light, and your judgment as the noonday. Rest in the LORD and wait patiently for Him.

**[135] ROMANS 8**

26 And in the same way the Spirit also helps our weakness; for we do not know how to pray as we should, but the Spirit Himself intercedes for us with groanings too deep for words.

When we try to "talk" someone into the kingdom, we merely lead them to an intellectual assent or an emotional response that will have no lasting foundation. Faith that will endure rests on the work of the Spirit and the power of God. That being the case, our efforts are far better spent interceding in prayer for our loved ones. We should ask God to extend His power to open their eyes to their own sin, convict them by His Spirit to the point of repentance (mourning and turning away from their old ways of life), and reveal Himself that they might fear Him. We should also ask God to appoint a "mouthpiece" to share the gospel at the appointed time when the Spirit opens their hearts to the revelation of God in Christ.

## LIMITATIONS OF WORDS IN PRAYER

We see the need for intercession and for prevailing in prayer. At the same time, we also realize the profound limitations of words (even in prayer) because we do not always know the heart of the Father. Such knowledge is needed to pray according to His will.

Read Proverbs 2:1-11 and John 15:7.[133] What two conditions must be met before God answers prayer?

- 
- 

When these conditions are met, what is the result?

Carefully read Psalm 37:3-7.[134] What does God promise to give us?

Apart from careful evaluation in light of the whole of Scripture, we might think that God has promised us a blank check. But on what does this promise hinge?

*If* we commit our way to the Lord and delight ourselves in Him and *if* we trust in Him and in His Word, He will cause our thoughts (our desires) to become agreeable to His will. When our prayers conform to God's agenda, our words are united with power. We can trust, then, that God will answer our prayers. To pray rightly, we must hear God's words, seek to understand them, and be diligent to hide them in our hearts. It's the internally abiding Word that inclines our ear toward God's wisdom, righteousness, judgment, and equity.

In addition to God's Word, what other resource does God give us for praying within His will according to Romans 8:26?[135]

The Spirit teaches us, comforts us, guides us, encourages us, and intercedes for us in unlimited expressions of the wisdom and power of God. In John 6:63, Jesus says, "It is the Spirit who gives life. The words that I have spoken to you are spirit and are life." Even when we don't have the right words to pray, we can pray rightly. The good news about the limitations of our words in the work of God's kingdom is that God's Spirit makes up what is lacking in our knowledge and understanding.

## BRINGING IT HOME . . .

1. What things have you been praying for over a period of time without seeing tangible answers or results? List them.


   Then ask these questions regarding each one:
   - Does this request contradict anything from God's Word?

   - Does this request come out of my desires or God's?

   - Am I trusting and rejoicing in God, regardless of His answers?

   - Am I willing to continue to persevere in prayer?

2. What decisions, if any, are you facing that make you feel inadequate due to lack of direction or knowledge? Bring each of these areas to God and express your feelings of confusion and lack of discernment. Then ask God to guide you in His Word and by His Spirit to make the right decision. Remember to thank the Holy Spirit for His intercession on your part.

## DAILY READING

Read Proverbs 24:21–25:28. Mark the verse that stands out most to you today. Select one of the verses you marked in this unit and commit it to memory.

*To the leader: As group members arrive, have each one write down one or two advertising slogans or catchy phrases. You will use this list in activity 3. Allow five or ten minutes to close this session.*

1. As a group, read Proverbs 27:6 and Matthew 18:15-17. Discuss the meaning of both of these passages and the best way to apply them personally and corporately (in the church). Divide into two groups and have each group discuss one of the case studies below. After several minutes, have the group share their comments with each other.

   - How would you apply the above verses to these situations?
   - At what point, if any, would you take the situations to other Christians?
   - Would exposing the truth be slander?

   Case Study 1: You and a fellow church member (Bob) are employed by XYZ Communications. Through the company grapevine you've heard that a laptop computer and several software manuals are missing. Then your boss tells you to be on the lookout for a computer with serial #1BZ2QR6. The next week you and your wife are at Bob's house for dessert. While the wives are preparing things, Bob takes you into the study to get a book you've been wanting to borrow. On his desk is a laptop computer exactly like the missing one. As Bob leaves the room, you check the serial number—unfortunately it matches the missing computer!

   Case Study 2: Your daughter Amy and her best friend Gayle often spend the night at each other's houses. When Amy returned home this morning, she was upset about something, but she didn't want to talk about it. Finally she came out of her room and said she needed to talk. She disclosed that Gayle's mom, Gloria, had her boyfriend, David, spend the night. And yes, they slept in the same bedroom. You've been friends with Gloria since before her husband's death five years ago. As a matter of fact you have been in several Bible study groups together and have just been asked to co-chair the next women's retreat.

2. Words have the power to build up or to tear down. It has been said that for every negative or destructive comment we receive, it takes ten positive statements to repair the damage. Compare and contrast the following pairs of words. Give examples for each one.

   Contention and Contentment
   Flattery and Encouragement
   Seduction and Self-Control
   Deception and Truth
   Gossip and Edification

   - What is the result of each type of speech or expression?
   - Who benefits and who is hurt or damaged?
   - Once the negative or evil words have been spoken, how can one repair the damage?

3. Evaluate all of the advertising slogans or catchy phrases that group members have written on the board. Use this scale: T = Truth, F = False or flattery, D= Deception, B = Seduction

   - What is the impact of these messages on you individually? On our society as a whole?
   - Who is most susceptible to these messages?
   - What "filters" or means of evaluating words do we need to have in place as Christians? Look back at each of this unit's Daily Excursions for scriptural input.

4. Share a time when someone exhorted (or corrected) you or when you exhorted someone else with positive results. Give the background or context of the exhortation, who spoke the words of correction, how the words were received, the impact of the words on both speaker and receiver, and the end result.

   - Why is it important to exhort one another in love (Ephesians 4:14-15)?
   - In what ways is timing important to speaking words that exhort (Proverbs 25:11)?
   - Have you had an experience with bad timing of words? Perhaps the words were true, but were not received because of when they were spoken. If so, share the example. What was wrong with the timing? When would it have been a better time?

Close by edifying and encouraging each other. Focus on each group member one at a time as all the other members share a word or phrase of encouragement with that person. Thank God for each person's uniqueness.

# INTRODUCTION TO UNIT 5
## WISDOM AND WEALTH

*Destination: To consider the principles that relate to the wise acquisition of wealth and the wise use of material possessions.*

Have you ever considered the real cost of the things we *think* we want and the wisdom of wanting them? I (Ken) vividly remember going to a friend's vacation house in the mountains. When I said to him, "I'd like to have a house like this," he replied, "Why? It's a lot of trouble and I let you use this one anytime you want." My friend's answer brought me up short, for my heart was really asking, *Why can't I have something like this?*

If most of us stopped to examine the real cost of ownership, we'd all have far fewer "toys." Not many make simplicity a goal, however, because we've bought into the lie that our worth is tied to the ownership of *things*. Rather than wishing for a vacation house, I would have been wiser to have simply thanked God for the abundance He had given to a friend and thanked my friend for wanting to share with me the pleasure of his posession without the bondage of ownership.

This last unit deals with wealth and wisdom. As we study this subject from Proverbs, we must keep in mind some of the truths mentioned in the introduction to this book. First, proverbs are totally valid, highly reliable, and typically repeatable life maxims—but they are not promises. Therefore, God is at liberty to orchestrate the unpredictable at any point in our lives without compromising His Word in any way. This is especially important to remember when studying money matters because unscriptural expectations can end in unwise disappointment with God.

The second thing we must keep in mind is that God's promise of material blessings as a reward for righteousness (things like rain, crops, children, or freedom from enemies) relate to His specific covenant with Israel, a theocratic nation. The Old Testament promises of material prosperity for righteous living should be understood, therefore, as a physical illustration intended to foreshadow the spiritual prosperity that would become ours through the righteousness of God in Christ. The Old Covenant promise of abundant fruit of the vine, for example, is a picture of the New Covenant promise of the fruit of the Spirit (love, joy, peace, patience, kindness, goodness, faithfulness, gentleness, self-control).

It is foolish, indeed, to make wealth our life goal. Wealth is fleeting; it cannot satisfy. Our first concern as Christians, then, is not adding to personal wealth but adding to God's kingdom. It will be helpful, therefore, to keep God's kingdom foremost in your thoughts as you study unit 5 on wealth and wisdom.

# DAY 1

## ATTAINING MATERIAL WEALTH

**136 JAMES 2**

5 Listen, my beloved brethren: did not God choose the poor of this world to be rich in faith and heirs of the kingdom which He promised to those who love Him?

**137 LUKE 3**

14 And some soldiers were questioning him, saying, "And what about us, what shall we do?" And he [Jesus] said to them, "Do not take money from anyone by force, or accuse anyone falsely, and be content with your wages."

**138 1 TIMOTHY 6**

6,8 But godliness actually is a means of great gain, when accompanied by contentment. . . . And if we have food and covering, with these we shall be content.
9-10 But those who want to get rich fall into temptation and a snare and many foolish and harmful desires which plunge men into ruin and destruction. For the love of money is a root of all sorts of evil, and some by longing for it have wandered away from the faith, and pierced themselves with many a pang.

Most of us think that those who attain wealth are more clever than those who don't. While cleverness is important, financial savvy alone won't produce wealth unless resources, markets, and even political climates are also favorable. And even then, God may withhold abundance. The fact is, attaining wealth has little to do with how hard we work, and wealth may reveal far more about our character than it does about our cleverness.

### WEALTH AS A MEASURE OF GOD'S APPROVAL

As mentioned earlier, some people believe that personal wealth is an indicator of God's approval or a measure of His love, based on Old Testament Scripture. However, consider James 2:5.[136] Whom did God choose to be heirs of His kingdom?

If God's approval appears to lean in any direction, New Testament Scripture would indicate it's toward the poor. But according to His Word as a whole, God isn't influenced by our wealth *or* our poverty. What matters to God is how our financial situation influences our attitude toward Him.[T36]

Read the prayer of Agur in Proverbs 30:7-9 from appendix A. Also read Luke 3:14[137] and 1 Timothy 6:6,8.[138] What must accompany godliness?

Both poverty and wealth present occasions for sin. The temptation in poverty is to steal and rail against God. The temptation in abundance is to either hoard it or become obsessed with the things money can buy. When our eyes are focused on our financial state, we will be discontent whether we are rich or poor. Discontentment plays right into the hands of the enemy. Read 1 Timothy 6:9-10.[138] What is the fate of those who make wealth their goal in life?

Note that it is the *love* of money (not money itself) that is *a*—not *the*—root of all kinds of evil. *The* root of all evil is pride. Nevertheless, the love of money leads to all sorts of moral compromise that offend the very nature of God. If we've made riches our goal in life, then we've made it a rival against God. Scripture calls that idolatry and spiritual adultery!

## ILL-GOTTEN GAIN

Read the following proverbs from appendix A and note what they teach about ill-gotten gain.

### Ill-Gotten Gain

1:10-19

10:2

13:11

22:16

28:8

28:16

God is concerned about our methods of attaining wealth and our use of whatever material abundance He allows. The love of money has incredible potential to lure us into obtaining wealth by immoral, unethical, or even illegal activities. While these activities may lead to wealth, Proverbs warns that ill-gotten gain will be costly in the long run. God is not against wealth, but He's against our acquiring it by any means that do not line up with His Word.

## ATTAINING WEALTH GOD'S WAY

Read Proverbs 10:4, 14:23, 21:5, and 28:19. How has God planned for us to increase our wealth?

Some people believe that work or labor is a curse resulting from Adam's rebellion, namely "Cursed is the ground because of you; In toil you shall eat of it all the days of your life. . . . By the sweat of your face you shall eat bread" (Genesis 3:17,19).

**POINT OF INTEREST:**[T36]
WEALTH IS NOT CONNECTED TO FAITH—First Samuel 2:7 says, "The Lord makes poor and rich; He brings low, He also exalts." Material wealth, then, comes from God. When God gives us abundant resources and we use them according to the principles in Scripture, then wealth is a blessing. This does not support a belief, however, that Jesus wants us to be rich (at least not materially). It also doesn't support the belief that if we give to certain ministries or have enough faith or live a good enough life that we will be materially prosperous. Scripture wants us to prosper, even as our soul prospers.

If we give from an attitude of "cashing in" on God's spiritual obligation of a high financial return, then we are attempting to use God as a celestial slot machine. If there were a connection between righteous living and material prosperity, then we would have to question the life and faith of the apostles and even of Christ. After all, Jesus said, "Foxes have holes, and the birds of the air have nests; but the Son of Man has nowhere to lay His head" (Matthew 8:20).

For both those who are amassing a lot of wealth and those who eke out a living, the impor-tant question is not "What did I do to deserve this" but "Lord, as steward of *Your* money, what do You want me to do with the resources You have placed in my care?"

**¹³⁹ GENESIS 2**
8-9,15  And the LORD God planted a garden toward the east, in Eden; and there He placed the man whom He had formed. And out of the ground the LORD God caused to grow every tree that is pleasing to the sight and good for food; the tree of life also in the midst of the garden, and the tree of the knowledge of good and evil. . . . Then the LORD God took the man and put him into the garden of Eden to cultivate it and keep it.

Go back to the chapter that precedes this passage and consider Genesis 2:8-9,15.[139] Did work exist before the Fall? If so, what was Adam's job?

God never intended for us to be idle.[T37] Idleness gives the enemy a foothold in our lives. Work, on the other hand, is our opportunity to interact with God's creation and to experience a measure of the creative process ourselves. The curse from Adam's sin was not the precipitator of work itself but of the stress, toil, and sometimes pain we experience as part of our work.

God expects us to work, accumulate wealth from our labor, be good stewards, and be diligent and prudent in handling our resources. God also wants us to practice moderation in our consumption by controlling our appetites for this world's goods and bringing our fleshly desires under subjection to His authority. When we yield the use of our resources to God and He increases our material wealth, then that wealth will be a blessing and not a hindrance to our walk with Him.

### WEALTH'S BENEFITS

Money or wealth is not a sin. Read the following proverbs and record some of the benefits of wealth.

10:22

13:22

14:24

19:4

Even if we give it all away, having wealth is having power. Wealth makes life smoother and easier for us, and it can be a defense against unforseen calamities (such as job loss or illness). As an inheritance, wealth can be an expression of forethought and care, providing financial security for the family from generation to generation. Wealth can even make us more popular, more sought-after than the poor. Though such seeking is superficial,

it nevertheless gives us the ability and power to influence things for good. Still, every benefit of wealth holds an inherent, potential danger. We'll explore these dangers in the remaining days.

## BRINGING IT HOME . . .

1. What is your basic view of money? Is it a necessary evil? God's blessing? A major goal of your life? Do a quick assessment of how you are handling what God has entrusted to you by reviewing your checkbook register. Where is your money going? For debts? For basic needs? For wants or luxuries? For the work of the kingdom?

   If an objective observer were to track your spending over the past six months, what would he or she conclude?

   Based on this simple look at your finances, what changes should you consider making? What changes in your lifestyle do you need to make in order to be able to adjust your spending?

2. As believers we are told to bear one another's burdens (Galatians 6:2). This can be applied to material needs. Is there anyone in your congregation who has a financial need you can help meet? For example, if you are an employer, have you considered hiring or offering personal training to a single parent to increase his or her earning potential? On the other hand, if you are in a position of true need, have you shared it with anyone else? Sometimes we go without because no one else knows what seems obvious to us.

### POINT OF INTEREST:[T37]

THE SLUGGARD—The sluggard is a tragic comic in Scripture. He's one who won't start things, finish things, or make any effort to fulfill his obligations. He has a million excuses not to go to work; and after a while, he starts to believe himself.

The sluggard's folly is laziness; and the result is a great lack of material things in his life. Sometimes in the Christian realm, laziness is disguised as spirituality. Professing to be a child of a providing Lord, some get the mindset that they should just trust the Lord for His provision. Ultimately, all that we have are God's provisions; but in His sovereignty, God has ordained that we should work. Never put a spiritual label on human laziness. God will not be mocked!

### DAILY READING

Read Proverbs 26:1–27:8. Mark the verse that stands out most to you today.

[140] **LUKE 12**

15 And He [Jesus] said to them, "Beware, and be on your guard against every form of greed [pleonexia]; for not even when one has an abundance does his life consist of his possessions."

[141] **1 TIMOTHY 6**

17-19 Instruct those who are rich in this present world not to be conceited or to fix their hope on the uncertainty of riches, but on God, who richly supplies us with all things to enjoy. Instruct them to do good, to be rich in good works, to be generous and ready to share, storing up for themselves the treasure of a good foundation for the future, so that they may take hold of that which is life indeed.

[142] **PHILIPPIANS 4**

11-13 For I have learned to be content in whatever circumstances I am. I know how to get along with humble means, and I also know how to live in prosperity; in any and every circumstance I have learned the secret of being filled and going hungry, both of having abundance and suffering need. I can do all things through Him who strengthens me.

# DAY 2

## WEALTH CANNOT SATISFY

We ended yesterday's study with the thought that while wealth offers some benefits, it still holds potential dangers for our spiritual well-being. One of those dangers is the belief that wealth will satisfy our longings. Nothing could be further from the truth! Either by direct testimony or by observation of their lives, we find emotional misery among the rich as well as the poor.

If anyone understood the limitations of wealth, it was King Solomon. We find Solomon's writings rather cynical toward the end of his days as recorded in Ecclesiastes:

> 2:11,17-20 Thus I considered all my activities . . . and the labor which I had exerted, and behold all was vanity and striving after wind and there was no profit under the sun. . . . So I hated life. . . . I hated all the fruit of my labor . . . for I must leave it to the man who will come after me. And who knows whether he will be a wise man or a fool? . . . Therefore I completely despaired of all the fruit of my labor.

> 5:10 He who loves money will not be satisfied with money, nor he who loves abundance with its income. This too is vanity.

Even in his writings in Proverbs, Solomon noted certain circumstances where people in poverty had an advantage over people with wealth. Read the following verses from Proverbs and note those circumstances or conditions.

| | Condition in Poverty | Condition in Wealth |
|---|---|---|
| 15:16 | | |
| 16:8 | | |
| 17:1 | | |
| 28:6 | | |

As we read from Ecclesiastes 5:10 (above), the love of money causes us to look for life satisfaction from a source that can only disappoint. Material wealth cannot meet our emotional and spiritual needs. Money can't buy

respect or joy or peace or love or any of those attributes that bring real quality to life.

Ironically, there are many accounts of emotional or relational upheavals brought about by the sudden gain of wealth (such as a large inheritance or winning the lottery). It is possible, therefore, for wealth to actually rob us of the life experiences that bring joy. It is far, far better to be lacking in this world's goods but having abundance in our relationships (both with God and others) than to be wealthy but unfulfilled—relationally as well as spiritually.

Read Luke 12:15.[140] Of what are we to beware?


Why?



Scripture tells us to be on guard not just against greed but against every form of it. We tend to think of greed only in terms of money, but the Greek word for "greed" is *pleonexia* (see Luke 12:15[140]). It means "gaining an advantage; coveting."[T38]

In the New Testament, wealth is often associated with the greedy, the oppressor, and the unbeliever—people who are so secure in their own riches that it's difficult for them to recognize their need of God except, perhaps, from a restless dissatisfaction with "things."

Read 1 Timothy 6:17-19.[141] What attitudes should the rich not exhibit? What should they be rich in?

- 

- 

Read Philippians 4:11-13.[142] What secret had Paul learned?



What was Paul's source of strength?

## LANGUAGE & LIT:[T38]

ALL FORMS OF GREED—
Our Western concept of greed has to do primarily with money and material possessions. Webster's Dictionary describes its English meaning as "excessive or reprehensible acquisitiveness." But the Greek word for greed has a much broader meaning—one that encompasses every form of unbridled desire. In addition to material wealth, this desire may be for power, prestige, social stand-ing, control, recognition, success, or any number of circumstances that puts a man or woman in a position of "one-upmanship" over another.

Ephesians 4:19 illustrates another form of greed when it speaks of people having "given themselves over to sensuality, for the practice of every kind of impurity with greediness." An insatiable desire for the unholy and profane—things like drugs, alcohol, illicit sex, and homo-sexuality—is another form of greed. Therefore, when we con-sider the full range of human tendencies that can be considered "greed," we will likely be con-victed. Colossians 3:5,[145] which links greed to idolatry, may apply to other areas of our lives far beyond a desire for wealth and materialism.

**143 NUMBERS 11**

1,4-6,33-34 Now the people became like those who complain of adversity in the hearing of the LORD; and when the LORD heard it, His anger was kindled. . . . And the rabble who were among them had greedy desires; and also the sons of Israel wept again and said, "Who will give us meat to eat? We remember the fish which we used to eat free in Egypt, the cucumbers and the melons and the leeks and the onions and the garlic, but now our appetite is gone. There is nothing at all to look at except this manna." While the meat was still between their teeth, before it was chewed, the anger of the LORD was kindled against the people, and the LORD struck the people with a very severe plague. So the name of that place was called Kibroth-hattaavah, because there they buried the people who had been greedy.

**144 EPHESIANS 5**

5 For this you know with certainty, that no immoral or impure person or covetous man, who is an idolater, has an inheritance in the kingdom of Christ and God.

**145 COLOSSIANS 3**

5 Therefore consider the members of your earthly body as dead to immorality, impurity, passion, evil desire, and greed, which amounts to idolatry.

**146 MATTHEW 16**

26 "For what will a man be profited, if he gains the whole world, and forfeits his soul? Or what will a man give in exchange for his soul?"

Paul tells us that godliness *with contentment* is great gain. Contentment doesn't mean we've resigned ourselves to poverty; it means we're resting in our situation in the midst of hard, honest labor and good stewardship. Contentment also means that we're truly thankful for the things we have and that we call those things "good."[T39]

There are any number of false expectations that can disappoint us, but greed will always be a source of discontentment. Greed is like a gnawing hunger that can never be satisfied because it focuses on whatever is lacking (real or imagined). As soon as the thing desired is obtained, greed immediately focuses on desiring something else. Even in the midst of abundance, then, greed will keep robbing us of joy. To the one for whom little is not enough, *nothing* is enough.

Being dissatisfied with God's provision is an affront to Him. Read of His reaction to whiners in Numbers 11:1,4-6,33-34.[143] What were the people doing in the hearing of the Lord?

What desires did the rabble among them have?

What was the Lord's reaction?

Who was buried at Kibroth-hattaavah? What was their cause of death?

God was not upset with the people for taking their desires to Him but for being unappreciative of His provision. Complaining to God over ligitimate suffering is a different issue. David said in Psalm 55:17, "Evening and morning and at noon, I will complain and murmur, and He will hear my voice." But David was in true adversity, in a battle not of his own making. In Numbers 11, the children of Israel became *like* those who complain of adversity, although they were experiencing only self-centeredness and greed—not adversity.

Read Proverbs 11:6 and 28:20,22. How does Solomon describe those who are caught by greed and who hasten after wealth?

What is their fate?

Because it always pushes the envelope of desire, greed is the force behind chasing after wealth. Greed undermines the Spirit of God and leads to sin.

Read Ephesians 5:5.[144] What will the covetous man lack?

According to Colossians 3:5,[145] what is greed equivalent to?

We've seen from Scripture that people who hasten after material wealth *as an end in itself* are headed for heartache and despair. We've seen that wealth cannot satisfy and that greed leads to sin and destruction. Proverbs tells us, therefore, to pursue character and peace and joy instead of wealth. A poor person with integrity is better off than the one who has low character and all that this world provides.

If you're still not convinced, however, read Matthew 16:26.[146] How would you answer the questions it asks?

**POINT OF INTEREST:**[T39]

BEING CONTENT—It's amazing how quickly the enemy can draw us off course in the area of contentment. I (Ken) have just come through a process where I was getting anxious over things related to provision. In spite of the fact that God has always abundantly provided in the past, I struggled because I had gotten my eyes on what I didn't have instead of what I did have. For a brief period, I lost my contentment and my peace.

In our materialistic world, it's so easy to get our eyes on the things that we perceive we lack. In truth, we're probably doing extremely well, especially compared to most people in this world and to most people who have ever lived. We'll have to maintain God's perspective if we expect to be content.

**BRINGING IT HOME . . .**

1. Only you and the Lord really know how contented you are with His provisions in your life. If this is an area of struggle, first be honest with yourself and with the Lord. Ask Him to reveal to you what legitimate needs you may be trying to meet with things of this world instead of things of the kingdom. Confess all that He shows you. Then ask Him to help you begin to have the mind of Christ in these areas.

2. Contentment is merely being grateful for all that you do have—no matter how great or small. Begin making a list of all God's provisions. Then express your contentment with a time of praise for what He has done for you—materially and spiritually.

**DAILY READING**

Read Proverbs 27:9–28:15. Mark the verse that stands out most to you today.

# DAY 3

## WEALTH IS FLEETING

An aspect of wealth we rarely consider is its temporary nature. In Proverbs 23:4-5 Solomon warns, do not "weary yourself to gain wealth, cease from your consideration of it. When you set your eyes on it, it is gone. For wealth certainly makes itself wings, like an eagle that flies toward the heavens."

Most of us have experienced this proverb firsthand. Part of our earnings are gone before we even see our paycheck. We pay our bills, perhaps put a little in savings, and . . . it's all gone. Our wages vanish for many reasons, but some common causes of "holes" through which wealth is lost are:

- Neglecting to work and produce income
- Mismanaging the money we have
- Failing to provide for the poor
- Failing to give back to God for the work of His kingdom

We'll look at the first three causes of vanishing wealth in this session and at the fourth cause on day 4.

### LAZINESS AND FINANCIAL NEGLIGENCE

The following verses from Proverbs address the impact of laziness and negligence on material wealth. Read them and write down your findings.

#### Effects of Laziness and Negligence

10:4

13:4

18:9

20:13

21:25

Read 1 Thessalonians 4:10-11[147] and 2 Thessalonians 3:10.[148] What do these passages tell us about our responsibility to work?

---

**[147] 1 THESSALONIANS 4**

10-11  But we urge you, brethren, to excel still more, and to make it your ambition to lead a quiet life and attend to your own business and work with your hands.

**[148] 2 THESSALONIANS 3**

10  If anyone will not work, neither let him eat.

**[149] ECCLESIASTES 9**

10  Whatever your hand finds to do, verily, do it with all your might.

**[150] COLOSSIANS 3**

22-24  Slaves, in all things obey those who are your masters on earth, not with external service, as those who merely please men, but with sincerity of heart, fearing the Lord. Whatever you do, do your work heartily, as for the Lord rather than for men; knowing that from the Lord you will receive the reward of the inheritance. It is the Lord Christ whom you serve.

Read Ecclesiastes 9:10[149] and Colossians 3:22-24.[150] To what degree should we apply ourselves to our work?

God also expects us to work and to work diligently—even heartily, with all our might! If we would strive for excellence in the *process* of our work (working as for the Lord) and leave the product or the outcome up to God, what do you think would happen to the stress of our work?

## POOR MANAGEMENT OF FINANCES

According to Proverbs 20:4 and 24:27, what is the sequence of activity required for making provision for ourselves and our families?

Failing to set priorities and failing to respond to timely opportunities are ways we somewhat passively mismanage our finances. Some ways we actively mismanage our money are becoming surety and gambling.[T40] "Surety" in Hebrew is *arab*. It means "to take on pledge or give in pledge." Becoming surety means putting oneself into financial obligation without the resources to do so. It involves being attracted to a deal, usually speculative, and then committing beyond one's possible ability to repay. Some think being surety is similar to co-signing a financial note. Read the following proverbs. Write what you learn about the pitfalls of becoming surety.

### Dangers of Surety

11:15

17:18

22:26-27

While we should give liberally, we shouldn't obligate ourselves for someone else's debt unless we have excess

**POINT OF INTEREST:[T40]**
WHAT'S "WRONG" WITH GAMBLING—You can't prove that gambling violates Scripture directly, but gambling certainly negates a number of biblical principles of God's call for financial responsibility. Lotteries, for example, are schemes to get rich quick at other people's expense. Lotteries often appeal to those who can least afford it; desperate people get sucked into hope against irrational odds.

We try to rationalize lotteries by coming up with some social benefit (usually education) or increased tax base, but even secular society is providing good arguments that lotteries are counterproductive for society as a whole. Gambling addictions and bankruptcies have increased dramatically as states have legalized gambling.

There are other things you have to consider, both as a Christian and as a responsible citizen; namely, where does this money really go, what kinds of businesses and social ills are associated with gambling, and would God be pleased that you were a participant in those activities?

Here is a good application of W.W.J.D. (What Would Jesus Do). If you think Jesus wouldn't go to a casino or buy a lottery ticket, you shouldn't either. (Before you answer, study the character of Jesus in the Gospels.)

**¹⁵¹ ECCLESIASTES 9**

11 I again saw under the sun that the race is not to the swift, and the battle is not to the warriors, and neither is bread to the wise, nor wealth to the discerning, nor favor to men of ability; for time and chance overtake them all.

**¹⁵² ECCLESIASTES 4**

8 There was a certain man without a dependent, having neither a son nor a brother, yet there was no end to all his labor. Indeed, his eyes were not satisfied with riches and he never asked, "And for whom am I laboring and depriving myself of pleasure?" This too is vanity and it is a grievous task.

resources that we are prepared to lose and unless we are assured of the Lord's leading in this area.

Proverbs 21:17,20 shows us the most common way people actively lose wealth. In summary, what is it?

We cannot build wealth and consume it at the same time. Attaining wealth requires us to bring our physical and material appetites, our personal goals, and our personal income in line with God's Word.

## FAILURE TO PROVIDE FOR THE POOR

Wealth is a trial of our faith. It's actually a far greater trial than is poverty because with poverty our desperate dependence on God is crystal clear—we are without resources. Wealth, on the other hand, creates the delusion that we are self-sufficient and superior to others. If God has given you an abundance of wealth, do not fall into the trap of thinking it is all for your enjoyment.

Read the following proverbs. Note what you learn about providing for the poor.

### Providing for the Poor

14:21

21:13

22:9

22:16

Superiority makes us look with disdain at the less fortunate and condemn them. We think, *they should work harder or save more.* The real motivation behind such thinking, however, is usually justification for spending our wealth on our own lusts rather than using it to meet legitimate needs—our own and others'. A delusion of superiority will be costly, for the proverbs above can be summed up in the old cliche, "what goes around, comes around."[T41]

Review James 2:5[136] and then read Ecclesiastes 9:11.[151] Briefly summarize what you learn from these verses.

## WEALTH IS TEMPORAL; WE ARE ETERNAL

Read Proverbs 27:24 and Eccleasiastes 4:8.[152] How much of our wealth can we take with us?

How much money will the wealthy person leave behind? All of it! Money doesn't abide; only people and God's Word abide forever. Jesus tells us that our hearts will be wherever our treasure is. Therefore, we should be prudent enough to have our treasure in heavenly realms where it will never be stolen or fade away (Matthew 6:19-21). We will transcend this world's goods and go on to an eternal destiny. It is not wrong to seek profit; but if we make wealth our final goal, we are selling life for eternally worthless goods.

## BRINGING IT HOME . . .

1. If your efforts are not bearing financial fruit, then examine yourself before God. Ask yourself:

   - Am I seeking first His kingdom or am I seeking wealth as an end in itself?

   - Am I working diligently as for the Lord?

   - Am I wisely managing the resources I do have?

   - Am I sharing what I have with others as I am able?

   If, after examining yourself before the Lord, you find no hidden sin, then just keep working and being a good steward; don't be self-condemning if your finances remain marginal.

2. Prior to this session, what was your view of gambling and lotteries? Has your opinion changed or been challenged? In what way? Do you need to do anything different as a result? If so, determine to take action starting today.

### POINT OF INTEREST:[T41]

SELF-ESTEEM VS. SUPERIORITY—From time to time, I (Ken) have been given free upgrades to first-class accommodations because flights were otherwise full. You know what? Even though I didn't pay for the ticket, I've found myself feeling that I was just a little better than the poor peons in the back. How absurd!

It's easy to get wrong-headed about our worth, and it's especially easy when we have wealth and power. The feeling of superiority is often subtle in origin and slow in maturation; and sometimes it's hard to tell where we really are on that issue. Nevertheless, from time to time we must ask ourselves tough questions about our own pride and arrogance. That means that we have to mentally put ourselves in other people's shoes. We also have to be honest about how we would react to "us" or how outside observers might see us. When we stop asking these questions, we are in danger of losing our anchor into reality.

The more expedient (and the hardest) thing to do is to ask those who are closest to us to tell us the truth about the things they observe in us. We must also ask God to reveal wrong attitudes about our worth and ask Him to renew a right spirit within us.

### DAILY READING

Read Proverbs 28:16–29:27. Mark the verse that stands out most to you today.

# DAY 4

## OUR WEALTH IS NOT OURS

Let's begin today's study by reviewing the "celestial ledger." Read Psalm 50:10-12[153] and Haggai 2:8.[154] Who is the real owner of all of the world's wealth?

Read Ezekiel 18:4[155] and Colossians 1:15-17.[156] What is the relationship between God and people in the physical realm?

Now read Job 34:14-15[157] in light of the last sentence from the Colossians 1:15-17 reference. What work (relating to your very existence) is God the Son performing, even at this moment?

That we should call anything "ours" is foolish presumption. Everything comes from God, including our ability to make money and acquire wealth. God made our bodies. He owns our souls. He made our intelligence and gave us our abilities to learn and earn. He provided the fundamental resources we need to operate and create. God keeps us alive and healthy; and if He would withdraw His Spirit, we would become but cosmic dust.

According to these Scriptures, then, there's just no such thing as a self-made person. Job is a good example of a wealthy man who was also great in God's sight. Read Job 1:1-3.[158] Where would Job rank on the list of the "ten-most-wealthy" men in the east?

Job had enormous wealth. But in Job 1:9-19 we read that Satan secured God's permission to destroy all the material things that Job had. In one day his cattle, donkeys, sheep, camels, plus his children were taken from him. Read Job 1:20-22.[159] How did Job respond to his losses?

---

**[153] PSALM 50**

10-12 "For every beast of the forest is Mine, the cattle on a thousand hills. I know every bird of the mountains, and everything that moves in the field is Mine. If I were hungry, I would not tell you; for the world is Mine, and all it contains."

**[154] HAGGAI 2**

8 "The silver is Mine, and the gold is Mine," declares the LORD of hosts.

**[155] EZEKIEL 18**

4 "Behold, all souls are Mine; the soul of the father as well as the soul of the son is Mine."

**[156] COLOSSIANS 1**

15-17 And He [Jesus] is the image of the invisible God, the first-born of all creation. For by Him all things were created, both in the heavens and on earth, visible and invisible, whether thrones or dominions or rulers or authorities—all things have been created by Him and for Him. And He is before all things, and in Him all things hold together.

**[157] JOB 34**

14-15 If He [God] should determine to do so, if He should gather to Himself His spirit and His breath, all flesh would perish together, and man would return to dust.

**[158] JOB 1**

1-3 There was a man . . . whose name was Job, and that man was blameless, upright, fearing God, and turning away from evil. And seven sons and three daughters were born to him. His possessions also were . . . [such that he] was the greatest of all the men of the east.

What enabled Job to respond this way?

Read Luke 12:16-21.[160] Contrast Job's attitude about stewardship of resources with the attitude of the rich man in this parable.

| Job's Attitude | Rich Man's Attitude |
|---|---|
| | |

## STEWARDSHIP: OFFERINGS

Part of good stewardship is reinvesting portions of God's resources into His kingdom. Sometimes we don't do this because we are miserly and hoard God's resources. Hoarding is a strategy for living independently of God. Those who trust God will express that trust by giving liberally and generously. By our giving, we acknowledge that everything belongs to God and that our job is to direct His resources toward accomplishing His intents.[T42]

Giving directly to God's kingdom doesn't always mean giving to a church or Christian organization. Note an important use of our money from each of these Proverbs passages.

**Right Use of Money**

3:9-10

11:24-28

14:31

19:17

22:9

Now read the following parable of the king from Matthew 25:34-40:

> "Then the King will say to those on His right, 'Come, you who are blessed of My Father, inherit the kingdom prepared for you from the foundation of the world. For I was hungry, and you gave Me something to eat; I was thirsty, and you gave Me drink; I was a stranger, and you invited Me in; naked, and you clothed Me; I was

**POINT OF INTEREST:**[T42]
SELF-INDULGENCE—
Consumerism is now, more than ever, creating artificial needs for things nobody needed until somebody invented them. We buy them and then conclude, "How did I ever get along without one of these" or else "What did I want this stupid thing for?" Actually, we did fine without it; but it's amazing how becoming gripped by things is a one-way street.

For example, once we got a typewriter, we weren't going to write manuscripts with a pen anymore. Once we got a computer, we weren't going to use a typewriter anymore.

There's nothing wrong with progress. But we have to keep in mind the difference between necessity and "nice-ity." It's so easy to justify those things that we want and so difficult to tell the difference between our needs and our greeds.

**[159] JOB 1**

20-22 Then Job arose and tore his robe and shaved his head; and he fell to the ground and worshiped. And he said, "Naked I came from my mother's womb, and naked I shall return there. The LORD gave and the LORD has taken away. Blessed be the name of the LORD." Through all this Job did not sin nor did he blame God.

**[160] LUKE 12**

16-21 And He [Jesus] told them a parable, saying, "The land of a certain rich man was very productive. And he began reasoning to himself, saying, 'What shall I do, since I have no place to store my crops?' And he said, 'This is what I will do: I will tear down my barns and build larger ones, and there I will store all my grain and my goods. And I will say to my soul, "Soul, you have many goods laid up for many years to come; take your ease, eat, drink and be merry." ' But God said to him, 'You fool! This very night your soul is required of you; and now who will own what you have prepared?' So is the man who lays up treasure for himself, and is not rich toward God."

**[161] EZEKIEL 16**

49-50 "Behold, this was the guilt of your sister Sodom: she and her daughters had arrogance, abundant food, and careless ease, but she did not help the poor and needy. Thus they were haughty. . . . Therefore I removed them when I saw it."

**[162] 2 CORINTHIANS 9**

7 Let each one do just as he has purposed in his heart; not grudgingly or under compulsion; for God loves a cheerful giver.

sick, and you visited Me; I was in prison, and you came to Me.' Then the righteous will answer Him, saying, 'Lord, when did we see You hungry . . . thirsty . . . a stranger . . . naked . . . or in prison, and come to You?' And the King will answer and say to them, 'Truly I say to you, to the extent that you did it to one of . . . the least of them, you did it to Me.'"

God wants us to give to the work of His kingdom, but no arena for giving appears to be more important to God than giving to the weak and the poor. Both Proverbs and the New Testament are filled with verses that support the importance of caring for the needy.

Read Ezekiel 16:49-50.[161] What was the guilt of Sodom and what was their punishment for that guilt?

- 
- 
- 

There is no excuse in a land as rich as ours for anyone to go hungry, unsheltered, or unclothed. We are to give back to God freely and sacrificially from the good things He has allowed us to use. And we haven't given sacrificially, by the way, until it hurts; that is, until it affects our lifestyle.

## STEWARDSHIP: TITHES

In the Hebrew religion, the people were required to tithe from their crops and other earnings to support the poor and the alien, the Levites (including the priests), and the temple. The Hebrew word for tithe *[maaser]* actually means "a tenth." In addition, the people gave other offerings. If you totaled the annual giving from all the commandments in the Old Testament, you'd come up with a figure of over twenty percent.

Some Christians believe that because it is not mentioned as a New Testament commandment, a tithe is no longer required. However, the New Testament does command us to support the widows, orphans, aliens, strangers, and preachers and teachers of the gospel. In addition, we have churches to build and maintain, parachurch ministries to support, and missionaries to send out. The absence of a command for "a tenth" in the New Testament, therefore, probably reveals the removal

of any percentage cap. New Testament directives tell us to give liberally, sacrificially, and proportionately as the Lord has prospered us. For most of us, that would be far more than a tenth. But the New Testament directive is less about how much we give and more about how we give it. Read 2 Corinthians 9:7.[162] What should be our heart attitude when giving back to God?

The percentage of how much one should give, then, can be best measured by the degree to which one desires to expand God's kingdom. How much is that for you?[T43]

## BRINGING IT HOME . . .

1. On day 1 of this unit you were asked to do a quick assessment of how you are handling what God has given you in terms of finances. Go a little further by asking yourself these questions:

   - What portion of my income and resources have I made available for His kingdom?

   - Have I done so out of obligation or gratitude?

   - Do I ever go without something I'd like to have or do in order to meet someone else's needs?

   - When was the last time I sought God's counsel in the area of finances?

2. Review the parable of the king from Matthew 25:34-40. Would you be among those on His right who were blessed because of their generosity and compassion for those who are in need of basic food and clothing, who are ill, or who are in prison?

   - If so, continue to meet the needs of others and ask God to guard your heart and mind from an attitude of pride or superiority because of your good deeds.

   - If not, seek God's will in the area of helping others. Ask Him for a sensitive and compassionate heart toward those in need.

### POINT OF INTEREST:[T43]

ATTITUDE AND GIVING— Giving is a direct reflection of where your heart (and thus your treasure) really is. In determining how much we give to the Lord, we should not be asking, "How much is enough to give" but rather "How much is enough to live on so I can maximize my giving?" If we don't set a cap on how much is enough to live on, then the answer will always be "I need just a little bit more." Investigate and pray before you give, but give heartily to the Lord.

Sometimes we do a better job of giving back financially than giving back with our time and talents. We give to organizations to help the poor or give to the poor through churches. This is a good thing, but it might not be the right thing. God may want us to invest *ourselves* as well as our money more directly in the life of a poor person or group of people in our circles of influence. Each of us should evaluate our own situation, of course, but sometimes it's too easy just to write a check (and sometimes a check is a temporary band-aid). Take these issues to God and ask Him to show you where, what, and how to give.

### DAILY READING

Read Proverbs 30:1-33. Mark the verse that stands out most to you today.

# DAY 5

## TRUE RICHES

In the last four Daily Excursions, we've focused primarily on material wealth. We learned that wealth is not a sin but that ill-gotten gain is sin that will bring pain. We also discovered that material wealth cannot satisfy—it is temporal and fleeting. Our life on this planet is less than a blip on the screen of eternity. It is foolish to spend our efforts pursuing something that can't be taken into eternal life and doesn't even satisfy in this one.

As we've already learned, the concept of true riches makes a dramatic paradigm shift from the Old Testament perspective to the New Testament perspective.

Read Hebrews 8:6-8,10.[163] At Calvary, what did Jesus become?

What would be different about the New Covenant according to Hebrews 8?

In about half of the New Testament Scriptures regarding wealth, "the rich" and "riches" are referred to in a negative sense. Unlike the Old Testament, no New Testament references indicate that material wealth is a sign of God's approval or blessing. Therefore, if the New Testament is a better covenant enacted on *better* promises, then the riches that are ours under the New Covenant must be better than the material wealth under the Old Covenant (prior to Christ). Read Romans 2:4[164] and Ephesians 1:7,18; 2:4-5,7[165] and write down the riches that are ours in Christ.

### Riches in Christ

Romans 2:4

Ephesians 1:7

Ephesians 1:18

Ephesians 2:4-5,7

The New Covenant offers us the kindness, forbearance, and patience of God. It offers us redemption and forgiveness in Christ. Through the New Covenant, we can receive the rich mercy and love of God; for in Christ, we are given eternal life and made heirs of the riches of

---

[163] **HEBREWS 8**

6-8,10  But now He [Jesus, Our High Priest] has obtained a more excellent ministry, by as much as He is also the mediator of a better covenant, which has been enacted on better promises. For if that first covenant had been faultless, there would have been no occasion sought for a second. . . . "BEHOLD, DAYS ARE COMING, SAYS THE LORD, WHEN I WILL EFFECT A NEW COVENANT WITH THE HOUSE OF ISRAEL AND WITH THE HOUSE OF JUDAH; . . . FOR THIS IS THE COVENANT THAT I WILL MAKE WITH THE HOUSE OF ISRAEL AFTER THOSE DAYS, SAYS THE LORD: I WILL PUT MY LAWS INTO THEIR MINDS, AND I WILL WRITE THEM UPON THEIR HEARTS. AND I WILL BE THEIR GOD, AND THEY SHALL BE MY PEOPLE."

[164] **ROMANS 2**

4  Or do you think lightly of the riches of His kindness and forbearance and patience, not knowing that the kindness of God leads you to repentance?

[165] **EPHESIANS 1 & 2**

1:7,18  In Him we have redemption through His blood, the forgiveness of our trespasses, according to the riches of His grace. . . .
I pray that the eyes of your heart may be enlightened, so that you may know . . . what are the riches of the glory of His inheritance in the saints.
2:4-5,7  But God, being rich in mercy, because of His great love with which He loved us . . . made us alive together with Christ . . . in order that . . . He might show the surpassing riches of His grace.

His glory. From the beginning, God intended to replace earthly wealth that will rust and fade away with uncorruptible, heavenly riches, as foreshadowed in the personification of wisdom.[T11]

Read Proverbs 3:13-26 and 8:1-21 from appendix A. To what is Wisdom's value compared?

What are her promises to those who find her?

Now compare your notes (above) with the Scriptures that follow:

**Romans 11:33:** Oh, the depth of the riches both of the wisdom and knowledge of God! How unsearchable are His judgments and unfathomable His ways!

**1 Corinthians 1:5:** That in everything you were enriched in Him, in all speech and all knowledge.

**1 Corinthians 1:30:** But by His doing you are in Christ Jesus, who became to us wisdom from God, and righteousness and sanctification, and redemption.

According to Solomon, "Wisdom is better than jewels; and all desirable things cannot compare with her" (Proverbs 8:11). Wisdom in the Old Testament is the foreshadowing of Christ in the New Testament. Through Him, we are enriched with the important things in life—the knowledge of God, wisdom from God, righteousness in God, and sanctification through God. The only wealth that will remain are the riches of God in Christ. If material wealth doesn't satisfy and is fleeting (as life itself is fleeting), then we should not be investing our lives in the pursuit of riches nor should we be excessively concerned about money to meet our needs. We can trust God to provide as He knows best.[T44]

**POINT OF INTEREST:**[T44]
WEALTH IS GOD'S CALL—
If God chooses to provide you with wealth, keep a right perspective. Remember, some people who are as "dollar-wise" as anybody else and work very hard still never do well financially. There are others who don't work nearly as hard and yet accumulate an abundance. God can provide a person with more of this world's goods if He chooses, or He can prevent all of his or her efforts from bearing material fruit.

Sometimes, the problem is a spiritual one. Consider the following Scripture from Haggai 1:6-7,9, "'You have sown much, but harvest little; you eat, but there is not enough to be satisfied; . . . he who earns, earns wages to put into a purse with holes.' Thus says the LORD of hosts, 'Consider your ways! . . . You look for much, but behold, it comes to little; when you bring it home, I blow it away. Why?' declares the LORD of hosts, 'Because of My house which lies desolate, while each of you runs to his own house.'"

Remember, the accumulation of wealth is really much less in our control than we might like to think. Also keep thanking God for the provision for your basic needs (which is all He has promised us). Wealth may be a hidden trap of pride and conceit or false security for you. God may withhold wealth for your own spiritual protection.

**166 MATTHEW 6**

31-33 "Do not be anxious then, saying, 'What shall we eat?' or 'What shall we drink?' or 'With what shall we clothe ourselves?' For all these things the Gentiles eagerly seek; for your heavenly Father knows that you need all these things. But seek first His kingdom and His righteousness; and all these things shall be added to you."

**167 PHILIPPIANS 4**

19 And my God shall supply all your needs according to His riches in glory in Christ Jesus.

**168 MATTHEW 13**

44 "The kingdom of heaven is like a treasure hidden in the field, which a man found and hid; and from joy over it he goes and sells all that he has, and buys that field."

**169 LUKE 12**

33-34 "Sell your possessions and give to charity; make yourselves purses which do not wear out, an unfailing treasure in heaven, where no thief comes near, nor moth destroys. For where your treasure is, there will your heart be also."

Read Matthew 6:31-33,[166] Philippians 4:19,[167] and 1 Timothy 6:17-19.[141] How are our needs really supplied?

What is it that we should be seeking?

How is this treasure described in 1 Timothy?

Working to provide for ourselves and our family is biblical. Working for wealth independently of God, however, is sin. Saving is biblical. Hoarding is sin. It's also foolish. The one who is greedy—the one who hoards—is like a person investing all he has in rainbarrels when he's within praying distance of Niagara Falls. There is an everflowing stream of provision from God for those who seek Him. We should be seeking His kingdom, devouring His words, and drinking from His vast provision.

Read Matthew 13:44.[168] What is God's kingdom like?

What was it worth to the man who purchased it?

What was the man's emotional state in response to his purchase?

Read Luke 12:33-34.[169] What will be located with your treasure?

The final warning about wealth is that it has a tremendous potential to draw our heart away and to keep us from knowing God as intimately as we might otherwise. If God grants us access to and/or control over His physical resources, you can be sure they are for the work of His kingdom and are not to be consumed by self-centered spending nor rendered useless through greed and hoarding. No matter how much money is in your hands, hold it up before God and seek His will on how you are to use it that it might earn for you true riches that will endure.

## BRINGING IT HOME . . .

1. What are the things you value most? One way to determine the answer is to look at how you spend your time. Record how much time you spent on these activities last week:

   - Work (job and home)
   - Recreation
   - Leisure
   - Relating (friends and family)
   - Relating with God
   - Service to others

   Overall do you have a good balance of meeting basic needs and investing in the kingdom? If not, on which activities did you spend too much time? Not enough time? Seek God's help in keeping the focus on His true riches.

2. Look back over unit 5 on Wisdom and Wealth. What new thought or principle from God's Word stands out to you? How can you apply this new insight in your everyday life?

## IN SUMMARY . . .

Proverbs is a marvelous instruction book about life, even for men and women who have not personally received Jesus Christ as Lord. But the *art* of living well—the truly abundant life—is found only in relationship to Him. If you have not yet received Christ and would like to know more about the salvation experience, read through the information in appendix B.

   If you know Christ, then continue to grow in wisdom through a diligent study of His Word. Our goal is to help you gain a deeper understanding of God's Word by preparing additional studies in the GUIDEBOOK series. We invite you to investigate other titles in this series as well as other Bible studies made available to you by NavPress and other publishers of biblically sound study materials.

## DAILY READING

Read Proverbs 31:1-31. Mark the verse that stands out most to you today. Review the verses you marked as you studied unit 5. Select one to commit to memory.

*To the leader: You will use the board or flip chart in activities 3 and 5.*

1. Read 1 Timothy 6:9-10.[138] How is this verse often misquoted? How do we know if we "love money"? Brainstorm some possible criteria for evaluating our attitudes toward money and material things. Use the following verses:
   Proverbs 30:7-9
   Philippians 4:11-13
   1 Timothy 6:6-8
   Hebrews 13:5

2. Read the following statements and mark each as either true (T) or false (F). As a group, discuss each one using Scripture to back up your opinion.
   __Materialism is a rich man's disease.
   __It doesn't matter how hard I work, if God wants me to be wealthy, He'll prosper me.
   __Gratitude and greed cannot coexist.
   __Lack of contentment is a sin.
   __Most people would be happier if they had more money.
   __Wealth is God's seal of approval on a person's life. (A poor person may be just as materialistic as a rich person if "stuff" is the focus of his or her life.)

3. In day 3 of this unit we saw that money and material things are only temporary, but people and the things of God are eternal.
   - How can you invest in God's work? What criteria can you use to determine when and how much to give to various Christian ministries within your church and in the Christian community at large?
   - What opportunities exist in your church or community for meeting the needs of the poor? List these local ministries on the board or flip chart. Select one for your group to get involved with on an on-going basis.
   - What are the dangers of gambling? Discuss biblical reasons to avoid gambling and lotteries.

4. It's easy to say, "Everything I have is the Lord's." It's much harder to live as if this is true. Divide into three groups and have each group discuss one of the following scenarios. After a few minutes have each small group share its findings with the entire group.
   - A missionary family is on furlough and they need a car. You have a brand new four-door sedan, a two-year-old minivan, and a ten-year-old two-door coupe. Which car, if any, would you make available to the missionaries? Why?
   - You have worked for the same major corporation for twenty years. Due to downsizing you have been given the option to take another position at two-thirds your current salary or to find another job elsewhere. How would you pray? What do you do and why?
   - Your total household income has increased to over $100,000. How do you determine what portion of that income you retain for personal use and what portion is given to God's work?

5. As a group answer this question: What are our true riches in Christ? To find answers, have each group member select one of the units in this GUIDEBOOK to review. List all the findings and related Scripture on the board.

Close with a time of praise for each thing listed.

# APPENDIX A—

## READINGS FROM PROVERBS

### CHAPTER 1

[2]To know wisdom and instruction, to discern the sayings of understanding,

[3]To receive instruction in wise behavior, righteousness, justice and equity;

[4]To give prudence to the naive, to the youth knowledge and discretion.

[7]The fear of the LORD is the beginning of knowledge; fools despise wisdom and instruction.

[8]Hear, my son, your father's instruction, and do not forsake your mother's teaching;

[9]Indeed, they are a graceful wreath to your head, and ornaments about your neck.

[10]My son, if sinners entice you, do not consent.

[11]If they say, "Come with us, Let us lie in wait for blood, let us ambush the innocent without cause;

[12]Let us swallow them alive like Sheol, even whole, as those who go down to the pit;

[13]We shall find all kinds of precious wealth, we shall fill our houses with spoil;

[14]Throw in your lot with us, we shall all have one purse,"

[15]My son, do not walk in the way with them. Keep your feet from their path,

[16]For their feet run to evil, and they hasten to shed blood.

[17]Indeed, it is useless to spread the net in the eyes of any bird;

[18]But they lie in wait for their own blood; they ambush their own lives.

[19]So are the ways of everyone who gains by violence; it takes away the life of its possessors.

[20]Wisdom shouts in the street, she lifts her voice in the square;

[21]At the head of the noisy streets she cries out; at the entrance of the gates in the city, she utters her sayings:

[22]"How long, O naive ones, will you love simplicity? And scoffers delight themselves in scoffing, and fools hate knowledge?

[23]"Turn to my reproof, behold, I will pour out my spirit on you; I will make my words known to you.

[24]Because I called, and you refused; I stretched out my hand, and no one paid attention;

[25]And you neglected all my counsel, and did not want my reproof;

[26]I will even laugh at your calamity; I will mock when your dread comes,

[27]When your dread comes like a storm, and your calamity comes on like a whirlwind, when distress and anguish come on you.

[28]"Then they will call on me, but I will not answer; they will seek me diligently, but they shall not find me,

[29]Because they hated knowledge, and did not choose the fear of the LORD.

[30]"They would not accept my counsel, they spurned all my reproof.

[31]"So they shall eat of the fruit of their own way, and be satiated with their own devices.

³²"For the waywardness of the naive shall kill them, and the complacency of fools shall destroy them.

³³"But he who listens to me shall live securely, and shall be at ease from the dread of evil."

## CHAPTER 2

¹My son, if you will receive my sayings, and treasure my commandments within you,

²Make your ear attentive to wisdom, incline your heart to understanding;

³For if you cry for discernment, lift your voice for understanding;

⁴If you seek her as silver, and search for her as for hidden treasures;

⁵Then you will discern the fear of the LORD, and discover the knowledge of God.

⁶For the LORD gives wisdom; from His mouth come knowledge and understanding.

⁷He stores up sound wisdom for the upright; He is a shield to those who walk in integrity,

⁸Guarding the paths of justice, and He preserves the way of His godly ones.

⁹Then you will discern righteousness and justice and equity and every good course.

¹⁰For wisdom will enter your heart, and knowledge will be pleasant to your soul;

¹¹Discretion will guard you, understanding will watch over you,

¹²To deliver you from the way of evil, from the man who speaks perverse things;

¹³From those who leave the paths of uprightness, to walk in the ways of darkness;

¹⁴Who delight in doing evil, and rejoice in the perversity of evil;

¹⁵Whose paths are crooked, and who are devious in their ways;

¹⁶To deliver you from the strange woman, from the adulteress who flatters with her words;

¹⁷That leaves the companion of her youth, and forgets the covenant of her God.

## CHAPTER 3

¹My son, do not forget my teaching, but let your heart keep my commandments;

²For length of days and years of life, and peace they will add to you.

³Do not let kindness and truth leave you; bind them around your neck, write them on the tablet of your heart.

⁴So you will find favor and good repute in the sight of God and man.

⁵Trust in the LORD with all your heart, and do not lean on your own understanding.

⁶In all your ways acknowledge Him, and He will make your paths straight.

⁷Do not be wise in your own eyes; fear the LORD and turn away from evil.

⁸It will be healing to your body, and refreshment to your bones.

⁹Honor the LORD from your wealth, and from the first of all your produce;

¹⁰So your barns will be filled with plenty, and your vats will overflow with new wine.

¹¹My son, do not reject the discipline of the LORD, or loathe His reproof,

¹²For whom the LORD loves He reproves, even as a father, the son in whom he delights.

¹³How blessed is the man who finds wisdom, and the man who gains understanding.

¹⁴For its profit is better than the profit of silver, and its gain than fine gold.

¹⁵She is more precious than jewels; and nothing you desire compares with her.

¹⁶Long life is in her right hand; in her left hand are riches and honor.

¹⁷Her ways are pleasant ways, and all her paths are peace.

¹⁸She is a tree of life to those who take hold of her, and happy are all who hold her fast.

<sup>19</sup>The Lord by wisdom founded the earth; by understanding He established the heavens.

<sup>20</sup>By His knowledge the deeps were broken up, and the skies drip with dew.

<sup>21</sup>My son, let them not depart from your sight; keep sound wisdom and discretion,

<sup>22</sup>So they will be life to your soul, and adornment to your neck.

<sup>23</sup>Then you will walk in your way securely, and your foot will not stumble.

<sup>24</sup>When you lie down, you will not be afraid; when you lie down, your sleep will be sweet.

<sup>25</sup>Do not be afraid of sudden fear, nor of the onslaught of the wicked when it comes;

<sup>26</sup>For the Lord will be your confidence, and will keep your foot from being caught.

<sup>31</sup>Do not envy a man of violence, and do not choose any of his ways.

## CHAPTER 4

<sup>5</sup>Acquire wisdom! Acquire understanding! Do not forget, nor turn away from the words of my mouth.

<sup>14</sup>Do not enter the path of the wicked, and do not proceed in the way of evil men.

<sup>15</sup>Avoid it, do not pass by it; turn away from it and pass on.

<sup>16</sup>For they cannot sleep unless they do evil; and they are robbed of sleep unless they make someone stumble.

<sup>17</sup>For they eat the bread of wickedness, and drink the wine of violence.

## CHAPTER 5

<sup>3</sup>For the lips of an adulteress drip honey, and smoother than oil is her speech;

<sup>4</sup>But in the end she is bitter as wormwood, sharp as a two-edged sword.

<sup>5</sup>Her feet go down to death, her steps lay hold of Sheol.

<sup>6</sup>She does not ponder the path of life; her ways are unstable, she does not know it.

<sup>7</sup>Now then, my sons, listen to me, and do not depart from the words of my mouth.

<sup>8</sup>Keep your way far from her, and do not go near the door of her house.

<sup>12</sup>And you say, "How I have hated instruction! And my heart spurned reproof!

<sup>13</sup>"And I have not listened to the voice of my teachers, nor inclined my ear to my instructors!

<sup>14</sup>"I was almost in utter ruin In the midst of the assembly and congregation."

<sup>21</sup>For the ways of a man are before the eyes of the Lord, and He watches all his paths.

<sup>22</sup>His own iniquities will capture the wicked, and he will be held with the cords of his sin.

<sup>23</sup>He will die for lack of instruction, and in the greatness of his folly he will go astray.

## CHAPTER 6

<sup>12</sup>A worthless person, a wicked man, is the one who walks with a false mouth,

<sup>13</sup>Who winks with his eyes, who signals with his feet, who points with his fingers;

<sup>14</sup>Who with perversity in his heart devises evil continually, who spreads strife.

<sup>15</sup>Therefore his calamity will come suddenly; instantly he will be broken, and there will be no healing.

<sup>22</sup>When you walk about, they will guide you; when you sleep, they will watch over you; and when you awake, they will talk to you.

<sup>23</sup>For the commandment is a lamp, and the teaching is light; and reproofs for discipline are the way of life,

<sup>24</sup>To keep you from the evil woman, from the smooth tongue of the adulteress.

## CHAPTER 7

<sup>1</sup>My son, keep my words, and treasure my commandments within you.

<sup>6</sup> For at the window of my house I looked out through my lattice,

[7]And I saw among the naive, I discerned among the youths, a young man lacking sense,

[8]Passing through the street near her corner; and he takes the way to her house,

[9]In the twilight, in the evening, in the middle of the night and in the darkness.

[10]And behold, a woman comes to meet him, dressed as a harlot and cunning of heart.

[21]With her many persuasions she entices him; with her flattering lips she seduces him.

[22]Suddenly he follows her, as an ox goes to the slaughter, or as one in fetters to the discipline of a fool,

[23]Until an arrow pierces through his liver; as a bird hastens to the snare, so he does not know that it will cost him his life.

[24]Now therefore, my sons, listen to me, and pay attention to the words of my mouth.

[25]Do not let your heart turn aside to her ways, do not stray into her paths.

[26]For many are the victims she has cast down, and numerous are all her slain.

[27]Her house is the way to Sheol, descending to the chambers of death.

## Chapter 8

[1]Does not wisdom call, and understanding lift up her voice?

[2]On top of the heights beside the way, where the paths meet, she takes her stand;

[3]Beside the gates, at the opening to the city, at the entrance of the doors, she cries out:

[4]"To you, O men, I call, and my voice is to the sons of men.

[5]"O naive ones, discern prudence; and, O fools, discern wisdom.

[6]"Listen, for I shall speak noble things; and the opening of my lips will produce right things.

[7]"For my mouth will utter truth; and wickedness is an abomination to my lips.

[8]"All the utterances of my mouth are in righteousness; there is nothing crooked or perverted in them.

[9]"They are all straightforward to him who understands, and right to those who find knowledge.

[10]"Take my instruction, and not silver, and knowledge rather than choicest gold.

[11]"For wisdom is better than jewels; and all desirable things can not compare with her.

[12]"I, wisdom, dwell with prudence, and I find knowledge and discretion.

[13]"The fear of the LORD is to hate evil; pride and arrogance and the evil way, and the perverted mouth, I hate.

[14]"Counsel is mine and sound wisdom; I am understanding, power is mine.

[15]"By me kings reign, and rulers decree justice.

[16]"By me princes rule, and nobles, all who judge rightly.

[17]"I love those who love me; and those who diligently seek me will find me.

[18]"Riches and honor are with me, enduring wealth and righteousness.

[19]"My fruit is better than gold, even pure gold, and my yield than choicest silver.

[20]"I walk in the way of righteousness, in the midst of the paths of justice,

[21]To endow those who love me with wealth, that I may fill their treasuries.

[22]"The LORD possessed me at the beginning of His way, before His works of old.

[23]"From everlasting I was established, from the beginning, from the earliest times of the earth.

[24]"When there were no depths I was brought forth, when there were no springs abounding with water.

[25]"Before the mountains were settled, before the hills I was brought forth;

26While He had not yet made the earth and the fields, nor the first dust of the world.

27"When He established the heavens, I was there, when He inscribed a circle on the face of the deep,

28When He made firm the skies above, when the springs of the deep became fixed,

29When He set for the sea its boundary, so that the water should not transgress His command, when He marked out the foundations of the earth;

30Then I was beside Him, as a master workman; and I was daily His delight, rejoicing always before Him,

31Rejoicing in the world, His earth, and having my delight in the sons of men.

32"Now therefore, O sons, listen to me, for blessed are they who keep my ways.

33"Heed instruction and be wise, and do not neglect it.

34"Blessed is the man who listens to me, watching daily at my gates, waiting at my doorposts.

35"For he who finds me finds life, and obtains favor from the LORD.

36"But he who sins against me injures himself; all those who hate me love death."

## CHAPTER 9

1Wisdom has built her house, she has hewn out her seven pillars;

2She has prepared her food, she has mixed her wine; she has also set her table;

3She has sent out her maidens, she calls from the tops of the heights of the city:

4"Whoever is naive, let him turn in here!" To him who lacks understanding she says,

5"Come, eat of my food, and drink of the wine I have mixed.

6"Forsake your folly and live, and proceed in the way of understanding."

7He who corrects a scoffer gets dishonor for himself, and he who reproves a wicked man gets insults for himself.

8Do not reprove a scoffer, lest he hate you, reprove a wise man, and he will love you.

9Give instruction to a wise man, and he will be still wiser, teach a righteous man, and he will increase his learning.

10The fear of the LORD is the beginning of wisdom, and the knowledge of the Holy One is understanding.

## CHAPTER 10

2Ill-gotten gains do not profit, but righteousness delivers from death.

3The LORD will not allow the righteous to hunger, but He will thrust aside the craving of the wicked.

4Poor is he who works with a negligent hand, but the hand of the diligent makes rich.

11The mouth of the righteous is a fountain of life, but the mouth of the wicked conceals violence.

16The wages of the righteous is life, the income of the wicked, punishment.

17He is on the path of life who heeds instruction, but he who forsakes reproof goes astray.

18He who conceals hatred has lying lips, and he who spreads slander is a fool.

19When there are many words, transgression is unavoidable, but he who restrains his lips is wise.

20The tongue of the righteous is as choice silver, the heart of the wicked is worth little.

21The lips of the righteous feed many, but fools die for lack of understanding.

22It is the blessing of the LORD that makes rich, and He adds no sorrow to it.

24What the wicked fears will come upon him, and the desire of the righteous will be granted.

25When the whirlwind passes, the wicked is no more, but the righteous has an everlasting foundation.

28The hope of the righteous is gladness, but the expectation of the wicked perishes.

<sup>30</sup>The righteous will never be shaken, but the wicked will not dwell in the land.

<sup>31</sup>The mouth of the righteous flows with wisdom, but the perverted tongue will be cut out.

## CHAPTER 11

<sup>2</sup>When pride comes, then comes dishonor, but with the humble is wisdom.

<sup>3</sup>The integrity of the upright will guide them, but the falseness of the treacherous will destroy them.

<sup>6</sup>The righteousness of the upright will deliver them, but the treacherous will be caught by their own greed.

<sup>8</sup>The righteous is delivered from trouble, but the wicked takes his place.

<sup>9</sup>With his mouth the godless man destroys his neighbor, but through knowledge the righteous will be delivered.

<sup>10</sup>When it goes well with the righteous, the city rejoices, and when the wicked perish, there is glad shouting.

<sup>11</sup>By the blessing of the upright a city is exalted, but by the mouth of the wicked it is torn down.

<sup>14</sup>Where there is no guidance, the people fall, but in abundance of counselors there is victory.

<sup>15</sup>He who is surety for a stranger will surely suffer for it, but he who hates going surety is safe.

<sup>18</sup>The wicked earns deceptive wages, but he who sows righteousness gets a true reward.

<sup>19</sup>He who is steadfast in righteousness will attain to life, and he who pursues evil will bring about his own death.

<sup>20</sup>The perverse in heart are an abomination to the LORD, but the blameless in their walk are His delight.

<sup>21</sup>Assuredly, the evil man will not go unpunished, but the descendants of the righteous will be delivered.

<sup>23</sup>The desire of the righteous is only good, but the expectation of the wicked is wrath.

<sup>24</sup>There is one who scatters, yet increases all the more, and there is one who withholds what is justly due, but it results only in want.

<sup>25</sup>The generous man will be prosperous, and he who waters will himself be watered.

<sup>26</sup>He who withholds grain, the people will curse him, but blessing will be on the head of him who sells it.

<sup>27</sup>He who diligently seeks good seeks favor, but he who searches after evil, it will come to him.

<sup>28</sup>He who trusts in his riches will fall, but the righteous will flourish like the green leaf.

<sup>30</sup>The fruit of the righteous is a tree of life, and he who is wise wins souls.

## CHAPTER 12

<sup>1</sup>Whoever loves discipline loves knowledge, but he who hates reproof is stupid.

<sup>3</sup>A man will not be established by wickedness, but the root of the righteous will not be moved.

<sup>5</sup>The thoughts of the righteous are just, but the counsels of the wicked are deceitful.

<sup>10</sup>A righteous man has regard for the life of his beast, but the compassion of the wicked is cruel.

<sup>12</sup>The wicked desires the booty of evil men, but the root of the righteous yields fruit.

<sup>16</sup>A fool's vexation is known at once, but a prudent man conceals dishonor.

<sup>17</sup>He who speaks truth tells what is right, but a false witness, deceit.

<sup>19</sup>Truthful lips will be established forever, but a lying tongue is only for a moment.

<sup>20</sup>Deceit is in the heart of those who devise evil, But counselors of peace have joy.

<sup>22</sup>Lying lips are an abomination to the LORD, but those who deal faithfully are His delight.

<sup>23</sup>A prudent man conceals knowledge, but the heart of fools proclaims folly.

<sup>25</sup>Anxiety in the heart of a man weighs it down, but a good word makes it glad.

<sup>26</sup>The righteous is a guide to his neighbor, but the way of the wicked leads them astray.

## CHAPTER 13

<sup>1</sup>A wise son accepts his father's discipline, but a scoffer does not listen to rebuke.

<sup>4</sup>The soul of the sluggard craves and gets nothing, but the soul of the diligent is made fat.

<sup>5</sup>A righteous man hates falsehood, but a wicked man acts disgustingly and shamefully.

<sup>10</sup>Through presumption comes nothing but strife, but with those who receive counsel is wisdom.

<sup>11</sup>Wealth obtained by fraud dwindles, but the one who gathers by labor increases it.

<sup>16</sup>Every prudent man acts with knowledge, but a fool displays folly.

<sup>18</sup>Poverty and shame will come to him who neglects discipline, but he who regards reproof will be honored.

<sup>20</sup>He who walks with wise men will be wise, but the companion of fools will suffer harm.

<sup>21</sup>Adversity pursues sinners, but the righteous will be rewarded with prosperity.

<sup>22</sup>A good man leaves an inheritance to his children's children, and the wealth of the sinner is stored up for the righteous.

## CHAPTER 14

<sup>5</sup>A faithful witness will not lie, but a false witness speaks lies.

<sup>8</sup>The wisdom of the prudent is to understand his way, but the folly of fools is deceit.

<sup>9</sup>Fools mock at sin, but among the upright there is good will.

<sup>11</sup>The house of the wicked will be destroyed, but the tent of the upright will flourish.

<sup>15</sup>The naive believes everything, but the prudent man considers his steps.

<sup>16</sup>A wise man is cautious and turns away from evil, but a fool is arrogant and careless.

<sup>21</sup>He who despises his neighbor sins, But happy is he who is gracious to the poor.

<sup>23</sup>In all labor there is profit, but mere talk leads only to poverty.

<sup>24</sup>The crown of the wise is their riches, but the folly of fools is foolishness.

<sup>29</sup>He who is slow to anger has great understanding, but he who is quick-tempered exalts folly.

<sup>30</sup>A tranquil heart is life to the body, but passion is rottenness to the bones.

<sup>31</sup>He who oppresses the poor reproaches his Maker, but he who is gracious to the needy honors Him.

<sup>32</sup>The wicked is thrust down by his wrongdoing, but the righteous has a refuge when he dies.

<sup>34</sup>Righteousness exalts a nation, but sin is a disgrace to any people.

## CHAPTER 15

<sup>4</sup>A soothing tongue is a tree of life, but perversion in it crushes the spirit.

<sup>5</sup>A fool rejects his father's discipline, but he who regards reproof is prudent.

<sup>8</sup>The sacrifice of the wicked is an abomination to the LORD, but the prayer of the upright is His delight.

<sup>9</sup>The way of the wicked is an abomination to the LORD, but He loves him who pursues righteousness.

<sup>16</sup>Better is a little with the fear of the LORD, than great treasure and turmoil with it.

<sup>18</sup>A hot-tempered man stirs up strife, but the slow to anger pacifies contention.

<sup>22</sup>Without consultation, plans are frustrated, but with many counselors they succeed.

²³A man has joy in an apt answer, and how delightful is a timely word!

²⁵The LORD will tear down the house of the proud, but He will establish the boundary of the widow.

²⁸The heart of the righteous ponders how to answer, but the mouth of the wicked pours out evil things.

³¹He whose ear listens to the life-giving reproof will dwell among the wise.

³²He who neglects discipline despises himself, but he who listens to reproof acquires understanding.

³³The fear of the LORD is the instruction for wisdom, and before honor comes humility.

## CHAPTER 16

¹The plans of the heart belong to man, but the answer of the tongue is from the LORD.

²All the ways of a man are clean in his own sight, but the LORD weighs the motives.

³Commit your works to the LORD, and your plans will be established.

⁵Everyone who is proud in heart is an abomination to the LORD; assuredly, he will not be unpunished.

⁸Better is a little with righteousness than great income with injustice.

⁹The mind of man plans his way, but the LORD directs his steps.

¹²It is an abomination for kings to commit wickedness, for a throne is established on righteousness.

¹³Righteous lips are the delight of kings, and he who speaks right is loved.

¹⁸Pride goes before destruction, and a haughty spirit before stumbling.

¹⁹It is better to be of a humble spirit with the lowly, than to divide the spoil with the proud.

²⁰He who gives attention to the word shall find good, and blessed is he who trusts in the LORD.

²¹The wise in heart will be called discerning, and sweetness of speech increases persuasiveness.

²⁴Pleasant words are a honeycomb, sweet to the soul and healing to the bones.

²⁷A worthless man digs up evil, while his words are as a scorching fire.

²⁸A perverse man spreads strife, and a slanderer separates intimate friends.

³⁰He who winks his eyes does so to devise perverse things; he who compresses his lips brings evil to pass.

³²He who is slow to anger is better than the mighty, and he who rules his spirit, than he who captures a city.

## CHAPTER 17

¹Better is a dry morsel and quietness with it than a house full of feasting with strife.

⁴An evildoer listens to wicked lips, a liar pays attention to a destructive tongue.

¹⁴The beginning of strife is like letting out water, so abandon the quarrel before it breaks out.

¹⁸A man lacking in sense pledges, and becomes surety in the presence of his neighbor.

²⁷He who restrains his words has knowledge, and he who has a cool spirit is a man of understanding.

²⁸Even a fool, when he keeps silent, is considered wise; when he closes his lips, he is counted prudent.

## CHAPTER 18

⁹He also who is slack in his work is brother to him who destroys.

¹⁰The name of the LORD is a strong tower; the righteous runs into it and is safe.

¹²Before destruction the heart of man is haughty, but humility goes before honor.

¹⁵The mind of the prudent acquires knowledge, and the ear of the wise seeks knowledge.

## CHAPTER 19

¹Better is a poor man who walks in his integrity than he who is perverse in speech and is a fool.

⁴Wealth adds many friends, but a poor man is separated from his friend.

⁵A false witness will not go unpunished, and he who tells lies will not escape.

¹¹A man's discretion makes him slow to anger, and it is his glory to overlook a transgression.

¹³A foolish son is destruction to his father, and the contentions of a wife are a constant dripping.

¹⁷He who is gracious to a poor man lends to the LORD and He will repay him for his good deed.

¹⁹A man of great anger shall bear the penalty, for if you rescue him, you will only have to do it again.

²⁰Listen to counsel and accept discipline, that you may be wise the rest of your days.

²¹Many are the plans in a man's heart, but the counsel of the LORD, it will stand.

²⁵Strike a scoffer and the naive may become shrewd, but reprove one who has understanding and he will gain knowledge.

²⁷Cease listening, my son, to discipline, and you will  stray from the words of knowledge.

## CHAPTER 20

³Keeping away from strife is an honor for a man, but any fool will quarrel.

⁴The sluggard does not plow after the autumn, so he begs during the harvest and has nothing.

¹³Do not love sleep, lest you become poor; open your eyes, and you will be satisfied with food.

¹⁹He who goes about as a slanderer reveals secrets, therefore do not associate with a gossip.

## CHAPTER 21

⁵The plans of the diligent lead surely to advantage, but everyone who is hasty comes surely to poverty.

⁹It is better to live in a corner of a roof, than in a house shared with a contentious woman.

¹³He who shuts his ear to the cry of the poor will also cry himself and not be answered.

¹⁷He who loves pleasure will become a poor man; he who loves wine and oil will not become rich.

¹⁹It is better to live in a desert land, than with a contentious and vexing woman.

²⁰There is precious treasure and oil in the dwelling of the wise, but a foolish man swallows it up.

²⁵The desire of the sluggard puts him to death, for his hands refuse to work;

²⁶All day long he is craving, while the righteous gives and does not hold back.

²⁸A false witness will perish, but the man who listens to the truth will speak forever.

## CHAPTER 22

³The prudent sees the evil and hides himself, but the naive go on, and are punished for it.

⁶Train up a child in the way he should go, even when he is old he will not depart from it.

⁹He who is generous will be blessed, for he gives some of his food to the poor.

¹⁰Drive out the scoffer, and contention will go out, even strife and dishonor will cease.

¹⁴The mouth of an adulteress is a deep pit; he who is cursed of the LORD will fall into it.

¹⁶He who oppresses the poor to make much for himself or who gives to the rich, will only come to poverty.

¹⁷Incline your ear and hear the words of the wise, and apply your mind to my knowledge;

²⁴Do not associate with a man given to anger; or go with a hot-tempered man,

²⁶Do not be among those who give pledges, among those who become sureties for debts.

²⁷If you have nothing with which to pay, why should he take your bed from under you?

## CHAPTER 23

²³Buy truth, and do not sell it, get wisdom and instruction and understanding.

²⁴The father of the righteous will greatly rejoice, and he who begets a wise son will be glad in him.

## CHAPTER 24

⁶For by wise guidance you will wage war, and in abundance of counselors there is victory.

¹⁶For though a righteous man falls seven times, he rises again, but the wicked stumble in time of calamity.

²⁵But to those who rebuke the wicked will be delight, and a good blessing will come upon them.

²⁷Prepare your work outside, and make it ready for yourself in the field; afterwards, then, build your house.

## CHAPTER 25

¹¹Like apples of gold in settings of silver is a word spoken in right circumstances.

¹³Like the cold of snow in the time of harvest is a faithful messenger to those who send him, for he refreshes the soul of his masters.

¹⁵By forbearance a ruler may be persuaded, and a soft tongue breaks the bone.

¹⁸Like a club and a sword and a sharp arrow is a man who bears false witness against his neighbor.

## CHAPTER 26

¹²Do you see a man wise in his own eyes? There is more hope for a fool than for him.

²¹Like charcoal to hot embers and wood to fire, so is a contentious man to kindle strife.

²⁸A lying tongue hates those it crushes, and a flattering mouth works ruin.

## CHAPTER 27

⁶Faithful are the wounds of a friend, but deceitful are the kisses of an enemy.

⁹Oil and perfume make the heart glad, so a man's counsel is sweet to his friend.

¹⁵A constant dripping on a day of steady rain and a contentious woman are alike;

²⁴For riches are not forever, nor does a crown endure to all generations.

## CHAPTER 28

¹The wicked flee when no one is pursuing, but the righteous are bold as a lion.

⁶Better is the poor who walks in his integrity, than he who is crooked though he be rich.

⁸He who increases his wealth by interest and usury, gathers it for him who is gracious to the poor.

¹¹The rich man is wise in his own eyes, but the poor who has understanding sees through him.

¹²When the righteous triumph, there is great glory, but when the wicked rise, men hide themselves.

¹³He who conceals his transgressions will not prosper, but he who confesses and forsakes them will find compassion.

¹⁶A leader who is a great oppressor lacks understanding, but he who hates unjust gain will prolong his days.

¹⁹He who tills his land will have plenty of food, but he who follows empty pursuits will have poverty in plenty.

²⁰A faithful man will abound with blessings, but he who makes haste to be rich will not go unpunished.

²²A man with an evil eye hastens after wealth, and does not know that want will come upon him.

²³He who rebukes a man will afterward find more favor than he who flatters with the tongue.

²⁴He who robs his father or his mother, and says, "It is not a transgression," is the companion of a man who destroys.

²⁵An arrogant man stirs up strife, but he who trusts in the LORD will prosper.

## CHAPTER 29

¹A man who hardens his neck after much reproof will suddenly be broken beyond remedy.

²When the righteous increase, the people rejoice, but when a wicked man rules, people groan.

⁵A man who flatters his neighbor is spreading a net for his steps.

⁶By transgression an evil man is ensnared, but the righteous sings and rejoices.

⁷The righteous is concerned for the rights of the poor, the wicked does not understand such concern.

⁸Scorners set a city aflame, but wise men turn away anger.

¹¹A fool always loses his temper, but a wise man holds it back.

¹⁵The rod and reproof give wisdom, but a child who gets his own way brings shame to his mother.

²²An angry man stirs up strife, and a hot-tempered man abounds in transgression.

²³A man's pride brings him low, but a humble spirit will obtain honor.

## CHAPTER 30

⁷Two things I asked of Thee, do not refuse me before I die:

⁸Keep deception and lies far from me, give me neither poverty nor riches; feed me with the food that is my portion,

⁹Lest I be full and deny Thee and say, "Who is the LORD?" Or lest I be in want and steal, and profane the name of my God.

## CHAPTER 31

⁸Open your mouth for the dumb, for the rights of all the unfortunate.

⁹Open your mouth, judge righteously, and defend the rights of the afflicted and needy.

# APPENDIX B—

## GOD'S PLAN OF SALVATION

In America today, most people either do not know what it means to be saved or do not understand that salvation is something they urgently need. God's plan of salvation is good news only when we understand the really bad news: namely, that all of us have broken God's law and the consequences are eternally serious.[141] As a result of Adam and Eve's rebellion, something happened not just "to" them but "in" them that continues to have a residual effect on us—their descendants. It is as if Adam acquired *bad blood* that was passed to all generations. Our inherited sin nature places each of us at odds with a pure and holy God.

Without a *spiritual transfusion*, our condition will end in eternal death (hell).[142] Within the context of this bad news, the tremendous good news of the gospel is fully realized. Through the cleansing power of the blood of Jesus Christ, God has made a way of escape.

Because Jesus was God the Son, His death on the cross satisfied—made propitiation for—the sin debt for all people.[143] This means that the ransom price for your sentence of eternal death has already been deposited by Christ into your account.[144] Whatever amount you need to be reconciled to God is available to you through His Son—and through Him alone.[145] When you come to Jesus, He will require one thing—that you yield your life to be spiritually born anew in Him.[146] So how does one go about being born anew?

### 1. BEGIN WITH AN HONEST AND SINCERE HEART

God knows exactly where you are and what you think and feel about Him. Therefore, you're free to—indeed you must—tell Him the truth. If you're not sure God exists, tell Him. Then ask Him to reveal Himself to you that you may fully believe in Him. If you don't like

**[141] ROMANS 3**
23 For all have sinned and fall short of the glory of God.
**ROMANS 6**
23 For the wages of sin is death, but the free gift of God is eternal life.

**[142] ROMANS 5**
12 Therefore, just as through one man sin entered into the world, and death through sin, and so death spread to all men, because all sinned.

**[143] 1 JOHN 2**
2 And He Himself is the propitiation for our sins; and not for ours only, but also for those of the whole world.

**[144] ROMANS 3**
24-26 [We are] justified as a gift by His grace through the redemption which is in Christ Jesus; whom God displayed publicly as a propitiation in His blood through faith . . . in the forbearance of God He passed over the sins previously committed; . . . that He might be just and the justifier of the one who has faith in Jesus.

**[145] ACTS 4**
12 There is salvation in no one else; for there is no other name [besides Jesus] under heaven that has been given among men, by which we must be saved.

**[146] 1 PETER 1**

23 For you have been born again not of seed which is perishable but imperishable, that is, through the living and abiding word of God.

**1 PETER 3**

18 For Christ also died for sins once for all, the just for the unjust, having been put to death in the flesh, but made alive in the spirit.

**[147] 1 PETER 2**

2 Like newborn babes, long for the pure milk of the word, that by it you may grow in respect to salvation.

**[148] ROMANS 3**

10-12 As it is written, "THERE IS NONE RIGHTEOUS, NOT EVEN ONE; THERE IS NONE WHO UNDERSTANDS, THERE IS NONE WHO SEEKS FOR GOD; ALL HAVE TURNED ASIDE, TOGETHER THEY HAVE BECOME USELESS; THERE IS NONE WHO DOES GOOD, THERE IS NOT EVEN ONE."

**[149] 1 JOHN 1**

9 If we confess our sins, He is faithful and righteous to forgive us our sins and to cleanse us from all unrighteousness.

**[150] 2 CORINTHIANS 7**

10 For the sorrow that is according to the will of God produces a repentance without regret, leading to salvation; but the sorrow of the world produces death.

**[151] EPHESIANS 2**

8-9 For by grace you have been saved through faith; and that not of yourselves, it is the gift of God; not as a result of works, that no one should boast.

reading His Word or you think His principles are too demanding or you don't like going to church, tell Him. Ask Him to help you through your resistance and to create a desire to know Him through His Word and through His people.[147] Whatever it is that has kept you from coming to God—pride, fear, shame, guilt, anger, disappointment, unbelief, lack of knowledge—tell Him about it and ask Him to bring you to a place of acceptance of His will in your life.

## 2. CONFESS YOUR SIN AND ASK GOD'S FORGIVENESS

See yourself among the *all* who have sinned.[141] Don't get sidetracked by focusing on your good points or by comparing yourself favorably to others—even to Christians. Don't confuse religious habits, such as church attendance or Christian service, with evidence of your own goodness. When measured against a pure and holy God, all human righteousness is worthless. Agree with God's Word that you are a sinner, and acknowledge your failed efforts at being good.[148] Confess the specific sins you are aware of, such as pride, jealousy, prejudice, intellectualism, anger, rebellion, or anything you see in your life that is unlike Christ.[149] Ask God to make you aware of any hidden sins and convict you of sin until you are truly and deeply sorry for displeasing Him.[150]

## 3. RECOGNIZE THAT YOU CANNOT SAVE YOURSELF

Understand that you need Someone to do *in* you what you cannot do in and for yourself.[151] You cannot save yourself, call yourself to God, change yourself, or even *really* believe in God by your own efforts.[152] In fact, you can't even desire to come to God by your own intent.[153] But this is great news. It means that any flicker of interest you have toward knowing God is evidence that He is calling you personally to Himself. Your part is to respond to His calling and to yield to His rule and reign in your life. You can trust Him for He is interested only in your highest good.

## 4. WATCH FOR EVIDENCE OF CHANGE FROM THE INSIDE OUT

Don't try to be good. Instead look for changes of the heart—different attitudes, greater love, peace, kindness, joy that spill out in changes in behavior.[154]

Be intentionally introspective—the changes may be subtle at first. Be still before the LORD and allow yourself to sense His presence and His peace. Ask God to let others see changes in you as confirmation that He is at work in your life. If you sense no changes or see no evidence of the Spirit in your life, go back to God and ask Him to reveal anything that may be holding you away from receiving His gift of eternal life. Go through each of these processes again and tell God you will continue seeking Him until He enables you to seek Him with your *whole* heart that He might be found by you, according to His promise.[155] As you grow in your walk with the LORD, both your awareness of sin and your wonder at the Cross will increase.

Meditate on the Scriptures in the side columns. You may want to pray them back to God as *your* own words, from *your* heart. Be assured. He is waiting and He will answer you.

Note: When you pray to receive Christ, seek out a Bible-believing church for fellowship, prayer, Bible study, and accountability.

[152] **JOHN 15**
16 "You did not choose Me [Jesus], but I chose you, and appointed you, that you should go and bear fruit, and that your fruit should remain."

[153] **JOHN 6**
37,44 "All that the Father gives Me shall come to Me, and the one who comes to Me I will certainly not cast out. No one can come to Me, unless the Father who sent Me draws him; and I will raise him up on the last day."

[154] **2 CORINTHIANS 5**
17 Therefore if any man is in Christ, he is a new creature; the old things passed away; behold, new things have come.

[155] **1 TIMOTHY 4**
16 Persevere in these things; for as you do this you will insure salvation both for yourself and for those who hear you.

# BIBLIOGRAPHY

Boa, Ken and Larry Moody. *I'm Glad You Asked*. Wheaton, IL: Victor, 1994.

Kidner, Derek. *The Proverbs*. Downers Grove, IL: InterVarsity, 1994.

Martin, William C. *The Layman's Bible Encyclopedia*. Nashville, TN: The Southwestern Company, 1964.

McQuilkin, J. Robertson. *Understanding and Applying the Bible*. Chicago: Moody, 1983.

Precept Ministries. *The International Inductive Study Bible*. Eugene, OR: Harvest House, 1993.

Strong, James. *The New Strong's Exhaustive Concordance of the Bible*. Nashville, TN: Thomas Nelson, 1984.

Teasdale, Sara. "Wisdom" from *Collected Poems*. New York: Macmillan, 1994.

Tenney, Merrill C., general editor. *The Zondervan Pictorial Bible*. Nashville, TN: The Southwestern Company, 1974.

Vine, W. E. , Merrill F. Unger, William White, Jr. *Vine's Expository Dictionary of Biblical Words*. Nashville, TN: Thomas Nelson, 1985.

Zodhiates, Spiros. *The Hebrew-Greek Key Study Bible*. Chattanooga, TN: AMG Publishers, 1990.

Kenneth Boa writes a free monthly teaching letter called Reflections. If you would like to be on the mailing list, call: 800-DRAW-NEAR (800-372-9632).